国际中文教育武术技术推广系列教材
Wushu Techniques Textbook Series for International Chinese Educ...

U0679926

国际武术联合会
International Wushu Federation
中国武术协会
Chinese Wushu Association
北京体育大学汉语国际推广武术师资培训基地
Wushu Teacher Training Base for Chinese International Promotion of Beijing Sport University

刀 术
Broadsword

林小美　主编
陈泽韬　　译

北京体育大学出版社

策划编辑：佟　晖
责任编辑：潘海英
责任校对：赵红霞
版式设计：李　鹤

图书在版编目（CIP）数据

刀术 : 汉英对照 / 林小美主编 ; 陈泽韬译. -- 北
京 : 北京体育大学出版社, 2022.6
　　ISBN 978-7-5644-3661-2

　　Ⅰ.①刀… Ⅱ.①林… ②陈… Ⅲ.①刀术(武术) -
基本知识 - 中国 - 汉、英 Ⅳ.①G852.22

中国版本图书馆CIP数据核字(2022)第093116号

刀术

DAOSHU

林小美　主编
陈泽韬　译

出版发行：北京体育大学出版社
地　　址：北京市海淀区农大南路1号院2号楼2层办公B-212
邮　　编：100084
网　　址：http : //cbs.bsu.edu.cn
发行部：010-62989320
邮购部：北京体育大学出版社读者服务部 010-62989432
印　　刷：唐山玺诚印务有限公司
开　　本：710 mm × 1000 mm　　　1/16
成品尺寸：170 mm × 240 mm
印　　张：9.75
字　　数：172千字
版　　次：2022年6月第1版
印　　次：2022年6月第1次印刷
定　　价：100.00元

国际中文教育武术技术推广系列教材

组织机构

教育部中外语言交流合作中心

北京体育大学

国际武术联合会

中国武术协会

审定委员会

吴 彬　门惠丰　金肖冰

编写委员会

总 主 编：李士英

副总主编：高楚兰　佟 晖

分册主编：王二平　李士英　李英奎

　　　　　林小美　高楚兰

国际中文教育武术技术推广系列教材
《刀术》编委会

主　编：林小美

副主编：马　岚

编　委：何　英　余沁芸　马紫晨

示　范：马　岚

译　者：陈泽韬

目录 Contents

武礼篇

Wushu Etiquette

中华武术历史悠久，源远流长，内容丰富多彩、博大精深。源于中国，属于世界的武术运动，深受世界各国人民喜爱，已成为全人类共有的精神、文化财富。

Chinese Wushu (martial arts) goes back to time immemorial, and is well-established, long-standing, and profound. Originating from China, Wushu also belongs to the world, and is greatly admired by people all over the world; it has become a spiritual and cultural asset shared by all.

一、武 礼　　　　　Wushu Etiquette

"未曾习武先习礼"，武礼是中国传统的礼法之一。武礼现已成为在国际上一致采用的、具有代表性的、规范统一的武术标准礼法。

武礼的行礼方式包括徒手礼（抱拳礼、注目礼）、持械礼、递械礼和接械礼等。

"Before practicing Wushu, acquire relevant etiquette first." Wushu etiquette is part of China's traditional cultural rule of etiquette, and has become a common practice in the international Wushu community.

Wushu etiquette is represented by barehanded salutes (palm-fist salute; eye salute), weapon-holding salute, weapon-delivering salute, and weapon-receiving salute.

1. 抱拳礼 Palm-fist Salute

抱拳礼的行礼方式是：并步站立，左手四指并拢伸直成掌，拇指屈拢，右手成拳，左掌心掩贴右拳面，左指根线与右拳棱相齐；左掌、右拳胸前相抱，高度与胸平齐，肘尖略下垂，拳、掌与胸间距为20~30厘米；头正，身直，目视受礼者。（图1-1）

抱拳礼的含义是：左掌为文，象征和平，代表武德，寓意孝敬父母、尊敬师长、爱国敬业、诚信友善、仁爱感恩、谦卑简朴；拇指弯曲表示谦虚，寓意武术源于中国，属于世界，应虚心好学、永不自大。右拳为武，象征力量，代表武技，寓意尚武崇德、追求卓越、为国争光、为民服务。左掌盖在右拳上表示爱心、礼让、止戈为武。两手相合，表示习武者要文武兼备、内外兼修，五湖四海天下武林是一家，以武会友、友好团结，弘扬武学文化，造福人类。抱拳礼的寓意为和平、团结和友谊。

The palm-fist salute is as follows: stand with your feet together; the four fingers of your left hand stay straight together as an open palm, with the thumb bent and close to the index finger; the right hand forms a fist, with knuckles pressed against the center of the left palm, and the left palm's finger base line aligned with the right fist's metacarpophalangeal joint line. The fist and palm stay together 20-30 cm away from in front of your chest, with the tips of both elbows slightly drooping. Keep your head and body upright, and gaze at the one receiving the salute. (Fig. 1-1)

The palm-fist salute means: the left palm stands for erudition, symbolizing peace and martial ethics, and implying filial piety to parents, respect for teachers, patriotism, dedication, honesty and friendliness, benevolence and gratitude, humility, and frugality; the bent thumb means modesty, implying that Wushu originates from China and belongs to the world, and that those practicing Wushu should be humble and studious, but never arrogant. The right fist stands for martial arts, symbolizing strength and skills, implying the pursuit of virtue and excellence, glory for the country, and service to the people. The left palm is covered on the right fist to express love, comity, and truce.

The fist meets the palm to indicate that those practicing Wushu must be a master of both the pen and sword, in other words, to be well versed in both polite letters and martial arts. The world's Wushu community is a big family; Wushu is practiced to meet with friends, maintain friendship and unity, and to promote Wushu culture to benefit humanity. In short, the palm-fist salute symbolizes peace, unity, and friendship.

图 1-1　抱拳礼
Fig. 1-1 Palm-fist Salute

2. 注目礼　　　　　　　　　　　　　　　　　　　　　　　Eye Salute

注目礼的行礼方法是：并步站立，目视受礼者或向前平视，身体正直，以示对受礼者的恭敬、尊重。若表示答诺或聆听指教受益时，可微点头示意。

The eye salute is as follows: stand with your feet together; gaze at the recipient or look straight ahead; keep your body upright to show respect for the recipient. To respond to an eye salute, you can nod your head slightly.

3. 持械礼 Salute with a Weapon

持械礼是习练武术器械时行的礼节，礼仪内涵同"抱拳礼"。

（1）持剑礼的行礼方法是：并步站立，左手持剑，屈臂，使剑身贴前臂外侧，斜横于胸前；右手拇指屈拢，成斜侧立掌（或剑指），以掌外沿附于左手食指根节，高度与胸平齐，肘微下垂，目视受礼者。（图1-2）

Saluting with a weapon is an etiquette to follow when practicing a weapon, and means the same as the palm-fist salute.

(1) Salute with a sword: stand with your feet together, hold the sword in your left hand, bend your arms, and the blade is attached to the outer edge of the left forearm and diagonally across the chest. Your right palm (or sword finger) stays oblique with the thumb bent, and the palm's outer edge is attached to the joint of the left hand's index finger. This position is at the height where the chest is, with the elbows slightly drooping and eyes on the recipient. (Fig. 1-2)

图 1-2 持剑礼
Fig. 1-2 Sword-holding Salute

（2）抱刀礼的行礼方法是：并步站立，左手抱刀，屈臂，使刀横于胸前，刀身斜向下，刀背贴附于前臂之上，刀刃向上；右手拇指屈拢成斜侧立掌，以掌心附在左手拇指第一指节上，高度与胸平齐，肘微下垂，目视受礼者。（图1-3）

(2) Salute with a broadsword: stand with your feet together, hold the broadsword with your left hand, and bend your arms so that the broacsword is horizontal to the chest; the blade is slanted downward, with its spine attached to your forearm, and its belly facing upward. Your right palm stays oblique with the thumb bent, and the palm is attached to the first knuckle of the left thumb. This position is at the height where the chest is, with the elbows slightly drooping and eyes on the recipient. (Fig. 1-3)

图 1-3　抱刀礼
Fig. 1-3 Broadsword-holding Salute

（3）持枪礼的行礼方法是：并步站立，右手握枪端，屈臂于胸前，枪身直立，枪尖向上；左手拇指屈拢成侧立掌，掌心与右手指根节指面相贴，高度与胸平齐，肘略下垂，目视受礼者。

(3) Salute with a spear: stand with your feet together, hold the spear in your right hand, with the arms bent in front of the chest; keep the spear upright, with its tip facing upward; keep your left palm in an oblique position with the thumb bent; the palm is in

contact with the right hand's finger joints. This position is at the height where the chest is, with the elbows slightly drooping and eyes on the recipient.

（4）持棍礼的行礼方法是：并步站立，右手握棍把段（靠棍把1/3处），屈臂于胸前，棍身直立，棍梢向上；左手拇指屈拢成侧立掌，掌心与右手指根节指面相贴，高度与胸平齐，肘略下垂，目视受礼者。（图1-4）

(4) Salute with a stick: stand with your feet together, hold the handle of the stick with your right hand (1/3 of the handle), with your arms bent in front of the chest; keep the stick upright, with its tip facing upward; keep your left palm in an oblique position with the thumb bent; the palm is in contact with the right hand's finger joints. This position is at the height where the chest is, with the elbows slightly drooping and eyes on the recipient. (Fig. 1-4)

图 1-4　持棍礼
Fig. 1-4 Stick-holding Salute

4. 递械礼　　　　　　　　　　　　　　　　Weapon-delivering Salute

递械礼包括递剑礼、递刀礼、递枪礼和递棍礼等。

（1）递剑礼的行礼方法是：并步站立，左手托护手盘，右手托剑前身，使剑平横于胸前，剑尖向右，目视接剑者。

（2）递刀礼的行礼方法是：并步站立，左手托护手盘，右手托刀前身，使刀平横于胸前，刀刃向里，目视接刀者。

（3）递枪礼的行礼方法是：并步站立，双手靠近握枪于把段处，左手在上，两臂屈圆，使枪垂直于体前，枪尖向上，目视接枪者。

（4）递棍礼的行礼方法是：并步站立，双手靠近握棍于把段（靠棍把1/3处），左手在上，两臂屈圆，使棍垂直竖于体前，棍梢向上，目视接棍者。

其他器械的递械礼参照上述规范统一。

The weapon-delivering salute includes the sword-delivering salute, broadsword-delivering salute, spear-delivering salute, and stick-delivering salute etc.

(1) The sword-delivering salute is as follows: stand with your feet together, hold the cross-guard in your left hand, and support the front section of the blade with your right hand, so that the sword stays horizontal across the chest, with the tip of the sword pointing to the right and eyes on the recipient.

(2) The broadsword-delivering salute is as follows: stand with your feet together, hold the cross-guard in your left hand, and support the front section of the broadsword with your right hand, so that the broadsword stays horizontal across the chest, with the belly of the broadsword facing inward, and eyes on the recipient.

(3) The spear-delivering salute is as follows: stand with your feet together, hold the spear with both hands close to the handle, with your left hand on top and arms rounded; the spear stays vertical in front of your body, with the spear tip facing upward and your eyes on the recipient.

(4) The stick-delivering salute is as follows: stand with your feet together, keep your

hands close and hold the stick by the handle (1/3 of the stick), with your left hand on top and arms rounded, so that the stick stays vertical in front of your body, with the tip of the stick facing upward and your eyes on the recipient.

For the delivering of other weapons, please refer to the above-mentioned methods.

5. 接械礼   Weapon-receiving Salute

接械礼包括接剑礼、接刀礼、接枪礼和接棍礼等。

（1）接剑礼的行礼方法是：开步站立，左手掌心向上，托剑于递剑者两手之间，右手手心向下接握剑柄，目视右手，接剑。

（2）接刀礼的行礼方法是：开步站立，左手掌心向上，托刀于递刀者两手之间，右手手心向下接握刀柄，目视右手，接刀。

（3）接枪礼的行礼方法是：开步站立，两手虎口向上，上下靠拢，左手在上，靠近递枪者手上部接握，目视双手，接枪。

（4）接棍礼的行礼方法是：开步站立，两手虎口向上，上下靠拢，左手在上，靠近递棍者手上部接握，目视双手，接棍。

其他器械的接械礼参照上述规范统一。

The weapon-receiving salute includes the sword-receiving salute, broadsword-receiving salute, spear-receiving salute, and stick-receiving salute etc.

(1) The sword-receiving salute is as follows: stand with your feet apart; your left palm faces upward and supports the sword between the deliverer's hands, and your right palm faces downward and holds the hilt of the sword; eyes on the right hand when receiving the sword.

(2) The broadsword receiving salute is as follows: stand with your feet apart; your left palm faces upward and supports the broadsword between the deliverer's hands, and your right palm faces downward and holds the hilt of the broadsword; eyes on the right hand when receiving the broadsword.

(3) The spear-receiving salute is as follows: stand with your feet apart; the part of the hand between the thumb and the index finger faces upward; hands stay close, with your left hand above your right hand and the deliverer's hands; eyes on both hands when receiving the spear.

(4) The stick-receiving salute is as follows: stand with your feet apart; the part of the hand between the thumb and the index finger faces upward; hands stay close, with your left hand above your right hand and the deliverer's hands; eyes on both hands when receiving the stick.

For the receiving of other weapons, please refer to the above-mentioned methods.

二、武礼的应用　　　　Applying Wushu Etiquette

队长整队完毕，向老师报告时，师生均行"注目礼"。老师向学生说"上课！"，队长发"敬礼！"口令，学生行"抱拳礼"；老师看学生都行礼端正后，行"抱拳礼"答谢，落手立正；然后学生再落手立正。礼毕，授课开始。

授课结束，队长整队完毕，老师对本节课的整体情况进行总结发言后示意队长发"敬礼！"口令，学生行"抱拳礼"；老师看学生都行礼端正后，行"抱拳礼"答谢，落手立正；然后学生再落手立正。礼毕，老师向学生说"下课！"，老师和学生同时击掌，下课。

After the team leader lines everyone up and reports to the instructor, both the instructor and students salute with their eyes. The instructor says to the students, "Class!", then the team leader gives the "Salute" instruction, and the students perform the palm-fist salute. The instructor will make sure that all students are saluting properly and respond to them with the same position. The instructor then puts down his hands and resumes the position of attention; the students will do the same. After this, the session begins.

At the end of the session, the team leader again lines everyone up, and the instructor recaps on the session and then signals the team leader to give the "Salute" instruction. Then the students perform the palm-fist salute, and the instructor will make sure that all students are saluting properly and respond to them with the same position. The instructor then puts down his hands and resumes the position of attention; the students will do the same. After this, the instructor says, "Class dismissed", and gives students a high five before they leave the class.

2. 专业理论课   Theoretical Sessions

　　老师走上讲台，向学生说"上课！"，队长发"起立！敬礼！"口令，学生行"抱拳礼"；老师看学生都行礼端正后，行"抱拳礼"答谢，落手立正；然后学生再落手立正，队长发"坐下！"口令。礼毕，学生就座，授课开始。

　　授课结束，老师向学生说"下课！"，队长发"起立！敬礼！"口令，学生行"抱拳礼"；老师看学生都行礼端正后，行"抱拳礼"答谢，落手立正；然后学生再落手立正，队长发"坐下！"口令。礼毕，学生就座，下课。

The instructor walks up to the podium and says to the students, "Class!", and the team leader follows by shouting out "Stand up! Salute!" The students then perform the palm-fist salute. The instructor will make sure that all students are saluting properly and respond to them with the same position. The instructor then puts down his hands and resumes the position of attention; the students will do the same. The team leader then shouts out "Sit down"! After this, the students are seated, and the session begins.

At the end of the session, the instructor says, "Class dismissed". The team leader shouts out "Stand up! Salute!", then the students perform the palm-fist salute. The instructor will make sure that all students are saluting properly and respond to them with the same position. The instructor then puts down his hands and resumes the position of attention; the students will do the same. The team leader then shouts out "Sit down"! After this, the students are seated, and the session ends.

3. 武术比赛、表演等　　　　Wushu Competition and Performance

在武术测试、比赛时，运动员听到点名后应立即进场，面向裁判长，行"抱拳礼"或"持械礼"，待裁判长示意后，即走向起势位置；完成套路后，须并步收势，再转向裁判长行"抱拳礼"或"持械礼"，即可退场；赛后示分时应向裁判长行"抱拳礼"或"持械礼"。

在武术表演时，表演开始前和结束后，表演者应向主席台上的贵宾、前辈和观众行"抱拳礼"或"持械礼"。在武术的社会活动中，表演者受到介绍时应行"抱拳礼"示礼。在交流技术、切磋技艺时，双方也应行"抱拳礼"或"持械礼"。武林同道见面问候、告别时，也应行"抱拳礼"，以体现尊师重道，礼尚往来。

During tests or competitions, athletes should enter the arena immediately upon hearing their names called out, face the referee, and perform the palm-fist salute or weapon-holding salute; after the referee gestures, athletes should go to the starting position, complete the routine, stand at the finishing position, and then turn to the referee to perform the palm-fist salute or weapon-holding salute before leaving the arena. When the scores are announced, athletes should perform the palm-fist salute or weapon-holding salute to the referee.

When performing Wushu, before and after the performance, performers should do the palm-fist salute or weapon-holding salute to the distinguished guests on the rostrum, seniors, and spectators. On social occasions of Wushu, when being introduced, performers should perform the palm-fist salute to show etiquette. When exchanging techniques and discussing skills, both sides should perform the palm-fist salute or weapon-holding salute. When Wushu colleagues greet each other or say goodbye, they should also perform the palm-fist salute to show respect for the instructor and courtesy.

刀术概述

Overview of Broadsword

一、认识刀术 — Understanding Broadsword

刀是一种单面长刃的短兵器，是武术十八般兵器之一。刀由刀身、护手盘、刀柄、刀首等构成。刀身由刀面、刀刃、刀尖和刀背组成。手握的部位称"刀柄"。刀柄与刀身之间的圆盘称"护手盘"，亦称"刀盘"。刀柄尾端称"刀首"，顶端设一小环，用于系刀彩。

刀的起源很早，可以上溯到旧石器时代，最初的刀只是一种石片，一侧较厚一侧较薄。到新石器时代，同时出现了石刀、骨刀和蚌刀。原始人使用石刀狩猎或削刮，出现了最简单的刀术。

古人开始使用青铜兵器时，刀只是人们防身自卫的武器和观赏收藏的物品，在战争中兵家尚未钻研刀的砍劈与格挡的作用，故早期刀术未能在战争中发挥应有作用。钢铁问世以后，刀的制作工艺逐渐得到改善，对擅长劈砍挥杀的钢刀制作质量要求越来越高，刀也成为历来主要战争兵器之一。这时最常用的刀为"环首刀"，是一种实战性较强的短兵器，刀柄端带有金属环，金属环可起到平衡配重作用，又可系绳套挂在手上以稳定握持，还能坠挂饰物和刀穗等。随着锻造技术的不断发展，后又出现了横刀，延长了刀柄，使其变为可以双手使用的窄刃厚脊的长直刀。随着时代的进一步发展，刀术开始用于健身娱乐和竞技表演，将技巧动作融入兵器对打表演之中，既使刀术动作形象逼真，又使得表演情节丰富有趣。

刀术发展至今已成为武术套路比赛中的主要短器械项目，是历届世界武术锦标赛、各大洲际武术锦标赛以及各国武术锦标赛主要竞赛项目之一。刀术以其独特的运动方式深受海内外武术爱好者喜爱。

A broadsword is a short weapon with a single-sided long blade and is one of the eighteen Wushu weapons. The broadsword is composed of a blade, a cross-guard, a grip, and a pommel. The blade consists of a fuller, an edge, a tip and a spine. The grip is where you hold the broadsword. What's between the hilt and the blade is called the cross-guard, also known as the quillon. The tail end of the hilt is called the pommel, where there's a small ring for tying the broadsword sash.

Broadswords evolve from ancient knives and can be traced back to the Paleolithic Age. The original knife was simply a kind of stone flake, thicker on one side and thinner on the other. In the Neolithic Age, stone knives, bone knives and clam knives appeared at the same time. The primitives used stone knives for hunting or scraping, and the simplest form of knife technique appeared.

When the ancients began to use bronze weapons, knives were only weapons for self-defense and ornamental collections. During the war, the military strategists had not yet studied the functions of knives for slashing and blocking, so early swordsmanship failed to play its due role in the war. After the advent of steel, the production process of knives gradually improved, and the quality requirements for steel knives that were good at slashing and killing became increasingly higher, and knives also became one of the main weapons of war in history. At that time, the most common knife was the "Huanshou Knife", which was a short weapon with strong practicality; on its hilt end was a metal ring, which could balance weight, and be used for tying a rope sleeve that can be hung on the hand for a stable grip, or for hanging ornaments etc. As forging technology developed, the horizontal knife appeared later, and the traditional hilt was extended to be longer, making it a long straight sword with a narrow blade and a thick ridge, one that could be used with both hands. With the further development of the times, swordsmanship began to be used in fitness, entertainment, and competitive performances, and relevant techniques were integrated into weapon sparring for performance purposes, which not only reflected the vividness of swordsmanship, but also elevated the performance and made it interesting.

Broadsword play has developed and become a main short weapon sparring event in competitions of martial arts routine, and it is one of the major events of previous World Martial Arts Championships, various intercontinental Martial Arts Championships, and national Martial Arts Championships. Broadsword play is deeply admired by Wushu enthusiasts both at home and abroad for its uniqueness.

二、刀术运动特点　　Features of Broadsword Play

武术家常用"刀如猛虎"来形容刀的勇猛彪悍、雄健有力、刀法密集、灵活多变、节奏明快等特点。刀以劈砍为主，另外还有撩、扎、截、点、崩、斩、抹、带、缠裹等刀法。

Wushu practitioners often use "as fierce as a tiger" to describe a broadsword, which is characterized by valor, vigor, diverse and flexible techniques, and seamless flow of moves. A broadsword is mainly used for chopping and cutting, and there are other techniques such as upper-cutting, thrusting, slashing, downward poking, upward poking, hacking, smearing, deflecting, coiling and wrapping.

1.刀法清晰　　Precise Techniques

刀术的攻防主要体现在刀尖、刀背、刀刃及支配刀动的刀把之上。刀尖锐利主要在于扎，给予对手致命一击。刀背厚钝，主要用于防守对方进攻时所用的缠头裹脑的贴身近卫。刀刃薄利主要用于劈、砍、斩、撩等动作，可展现刀术的技击特征。把法遵循"把法变招，固把击法"的原则。刀术的每一种技法都有着严格的要求，不可混淆，只有遵从刀的构造、配合刀的构造原理，才能发挥出刀术的特性。练习者一定要做到路线清晰、力点准确、刀法分明。

The offense and defense of a broadsword are mainly reflected in its tip, spine, edge and handle. The broadsword is sharp and mainly used for thrusting, dealing the opponent a fatal blow. The spine of the broadsword is thick and blunt, and is mainly used for close-body defense when applying the wrapping and coiling techniques to protect yourself from the opponent's attack. The thin and sharp blade is mainly used for chopping, cutting, hacking, and upper-cutting etc., which show the technical features of swordsmanship. Broadsword practitioners should follow the principle of "turning techniques into moves and keep honing your techniques to counterattack". Each broadsword technique has strict requirements, which should not be confused. Only by understanding the broadsword structure can we bring it into full play. Practitioners must have a clear plan and exert force accurately with precise broadsword techniques.

2. 刀术尚猛   Fierce Swordsmanship

"刀之利，利在砍"，劈砍是刀的主要方法，必须刚猛有力才能奏效。因战斗的需要，为单刀规定了"刀术尚猛"的技法要求。对刀术的基本要求是"身法为要，偃跳超距，眼快手捷"。这里所说的"身法为要"，是指身法灵活多变，以躯干来带动刀的运动，以助刀的发力。"偃跳超距"是指跳跃轻灵，步法迅疾。"眼快手捷"是指眼法敏锐，挥刀快速勇猛。

"The sharpness of a broadsword lies in its being able to cut." Chopping and cutting are the main techniques, which must be strong and powerful to be effective. Due to the needs of combat, the technical requirements of "fierce swordsmanship" are stipulated for a single-handed broadsword. In the past, the basic requirement for swordsmanship was that "the practitioner's body should be flexible, and the torso be used to drive the movement of the broadsword to facilitate its exerting force; the practitioner should be able to jump lightly and have swift footwork; the practitioner should have sharp eyes and swing the broadsword valiantly".

3.刀手配合　　　　　　　　　　　　Broadsword-hand Coordination

拳谚讲"单刀看闲手，双刀看步走"。刀术练习，特别讲究刀的运动必须与不握刀的闲手（左手）配合密切。刀手配合，一是有助于躯干和四肢在运动中的和谐，二是有助于维持运动中的平衡，三是有助于刀法力量在运动中的发挥。这是刀手配合的三点原则。刀术的动作变化很多，要做到刀手配合密切，须根据不同的动作结构，运用三点原则使动作和谐、稳定、有力。

There is a proverb that says, "When performing with a single-handed broadsword, watch the idle hand; when with a double-handed broacsword, watch footwork." When practicing swordsmanship, it is especially important that the movement of the broadsword be closely coordinated with the idle hand (left hand) that does not hold the broadsword. The broadsword-hand coordination helps maintain torso-limb coordination and overall balance in the movement, as well as facilitates exerting force properly when applying the techniques. These are also the three principles of broadsword-hand coordination. There are many changes in the moves of swordsmanship. To ensure close broadsword-hand coordination, it is necessary to follow the three principles to make the movement harmonious, stable, and powerful according to different movement structures.

4.身械协调　　　　　　　　　　　　Body-weapon Coordination

刀术强调用整个身体来带动器械，"刀不离身左右前后，手足肩臂与刀俱转"，肩肘腕，足膝胯，以及胸腰，都须与刀法配合，身械协调。凡刀法所动，就应做到以身带肩、以肩带臂、以腕制刀、腰腿助力。例如，抢劈刀，须拧腰转体，右肩前顺，肩动而臂伸，腕随臂的挥动而转动，使刀的劈法借助于腰、肩、臂、腕的整体活动而将力量发挥出来。如果身腰不活，肩肘腕僵硬，不能形成整体活动，身械也无从协调，刀法也无从发挥。同一种刀法也可以有多种配合技巧，但要遵守有助于肢体在运动中保持稳固和协调，便于动作之间衔接使其对称美观，符合技击规律，同时协调身体与刀法的运动等总体规律。所以刀术练习讲究"以身法为要"，身械必须协调。

Swordsmanship emphasizes the use of the entire body to drive the broadsword. "The broadsword always stays close to the body (left, right, front, or back); the hands, feet, shoulders, and arms turn with the broadsword." The shoulders, elbows, wrists, feet, knees and hips, chest, and waist, must be coordinated with the broadsword. Whenever the broadsword moves, one should use the body to drive the shoulders, the shoulders to drive the arms, the wrist to control the broadsword, and the waist and legs to assist. For example, when using the broadsword to chop, one must twist the waist and turn the body, the right shoulder stays straight forward, the shoulder moves and the arm is extended, and the wrist turns with the swing of the arm, so that the power of chopping could be exerted by the overall movement of the waist, shoulders, arms, and wrist. If the body and waist are inflexible, and the shoulders, elbows and wrists are stiff, then an overall movement of the body is impossible, and there is no way to coordinate the body and weapon, and as a result, the broadsword can't function properly. A same broadsword technique can also have various coordination skills, but every coordination skill must follow a general principle: stabilize and coordinate the limbs during movement; facilitate the flow of movements to make them symmetrical and beautiful; conform to the law of combat; coordinate the body movement and broadsword techniques. In short, when practicing swordsmanship, one must pay attention to "using the body properly", and the body and weapon must be coordinated.

5. 刚柔兼用   Force Tempered with Mercy

刀术尚猛，但猛并不等于纯刚，刀法的运使强调刚柔兼用。一般说来，刀术中的防守闪避动作宜用柔，进攻动作宜用刚。例如，刀术的缠头裹脑、绕背的动作是防、避，宜柔；平扫斩击的动作是攻，宜刚。同时，在一个动作里，也须有刚有柔。例如，劈刀，起势时宜柔，落点时宜刚，没有起势时的柔，也就没有落点时所谓的刚。要做到有刚有柔的要求，必须明刀法、知攻守。

Swordsmanship is fierce, but fierceness does not mean pure force. Swordsmanship emphasizes both force and softness. In general, defense and parrying in swordsmanship should be soft, and the offense should be forceful. For example, the wrapping and coiling techniques are used for protection, and therefore should be soft; broadsword sweeping and hacking are used for attacking, and therefore should be forceful. For a single move, there must also be force and softness. For example, when chopping with the broadsword, one should be soft in the starting position, and be forceful when the broadsword falls. In other words, the softness in the beginning lays a foundation for the force in the end. To achieve the requirements of force tempered with mercy, one must be clear about the broadsword techniques and know how to attack and defend.

刀术基本动作

Basic Movements of Broadsword

一、持刀方法　　　　　　　　　　　Holding a Broadsword

1. 握刀　　　　　　　　　　　　　　Gripping a Broadsword

以右手为例。右手虎口紧贴护手盘，五指屈握刀柄。（图2-1）

要点：手腕要灵活自然，随刀法变化，适当调整握力。

Take the right hand for example. The part between the thumb and index finger stays close to the cross-guard, with fingers bent on the grip. (Fig. 2-1)

Key Points: The wrist stays flexible and natural; adjust the grip appropriately with the changes in the broadsword movements.

图 2-1　握刀

Fig. 2-1 Gripping a Broadsword

2. 抱刀   Resting a Broadsword

左手屈腕，食指与中指夹住刀柄，拇指压于护手盘之上，刀尖向上，刀刃向前。（图2-2）

要点：身体保持正直，挺胸抬头，刀身与身体呈一条直线。

Bend the left wrist, clutch the broadsword with the index finger and middle finger, and press the thumb on the cross-guard, with the tip of the broadsword facing upward, and the blade facing forward. (Fig. 2-2)

Key Points: Keep your body upright and your chest up, and keep the blade in a straight line with your body.

图 2-2　抱刀
Fig. 2-2　Resting a Broadsword

二、持刀礼仪   Etiquette of Holding a Broadsword

抱刀礼   Broadsword-holding Salute

并步站立，左手抱刀，屈臂使刀横于胸前，刀身斜向下，刀背贴于左臂，呈立抱刀式；右手为掌，以掌根附左腕内侧（刀身后部）；两手高与肩齐，距胸20～30厘米；目视前方。（图2-3）

要点： 两臂抱圆外撑，肘略低于手，目视受礼者。

Stand with your feet together, hold the broadsword in the left hand, and bend the arms to put the broadsword diagonally across the chest. The blade is slanted downward, and the spine of the broadsword is attached to the left arm; the base of the right palm is attached to the inner side of the left wrist (the back of the broadsword); both hands are at the shoulder level, and 20-30 cm away from the chest; look straight ahead. (Fig. 2-3)

Key Points: Both arms are rounded and extended outward, with the elbows slightly lower than the hands, and eyes on the recipient.

图 2-3　抱刀礼
Fig. 2-3 Broadsword-holding Salute

三、基本手型　　　　　　　Basic Hand Forms

1.掌　　　　　　　　　　　　　　　　　　　　　　Palm

掌四指伸直并拢，拇指梢节屈扣于虎口处（图2-4）。手腕伸直为直掌；向拇指侧伸，掌指向上为立掌。

要点：掌心突出，竖指。

Four fingers stay straight together, and the tip of the thumb is flexed and rests between the index finger and thumb (Fig. 2-4). A straight wrist makes a straight palm (zhi zhang) ; if the wrist is turned toward the thumb, it's called a standing palm (li zhang).

Key Points: Keep the hollow of the palm outward and fingers straight.

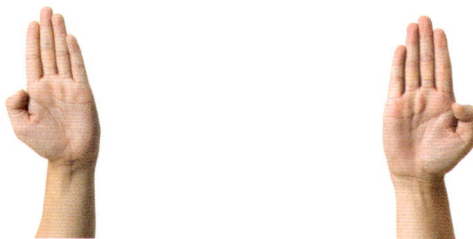

图 2-4　掌
Fig. 2-4 Palm

2. 拳　　　　　　　　　　　　　　　　　　　　　　　　　　　Fist

四指并拢卷握，拇指梢节屈压于食指中节上（图2-5）。拳心向上（下）为平拳，拳眼向上（下）为立拳。

要点：拳握紧，拳面平，直腕。

Fingers are held together, and the tip of the thumb is flexed and pressed against the middle of the index finger (Fig. 2-5). A fist with the palm facing up (down) is a flat fist, and a fist with the thumb and index finger facing up (down) is a standing fist.

Key Points: Keep the fist clenched and flat, and the wrist straight.

图 2-5　拳
Fig. 2-5　Fist

3. 勾　　　　　　　　　　　　　　　　　　　　　　　　　　　Hook

五指尖捏拢在一起，屈腕。（图2-6）

要点：屈腕要用力。

Pinch the tips of your fingers together and bend your wrist. (Fig. 2-6)

Key Points: Bend your wrist with force.

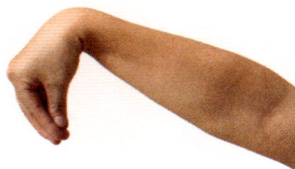

图 2-6　勾
Fig. 2-6　Hook

四、基本步型 Basic Stances

1. 马步 Horse Stance

两脚平行开立（约本人脚长的3倍），脚跟外蹬，脚尖平行向前，屈膝半蹲，大腿呈水平位，膝关节不超过脚尖，圆裆；目视前方。（图2-7）

要点：挺胸、立腰、直背，膝关节外撑。

Stand with your feet parallel and apart (about 3 times the length of your foot); keep your heels firm, and toes parallel and forward; bend your knees and squat, keep your thighs horizontal, and make sure your knees do not go over your toes; keep your crotch round; look straight ahead. (Fig. 2-7)

Key Points: Keep your chest out, waist up, back straight, and knees extended outward.

图 2-7　马步
Fig. 2-7 Horse Stance

2. 弓步 {Bow Stance}

两脚并步站立，两手握拳分别抱于腰侧，拳心向上；左（右）脚向前迈出一步（本人脚长的4～5倍），屈膝半蹲，大腿呈水平位，脚尖微内扣，膝关节不超过脚尖；右（左）腿挺膝伸直，脚尖斜向前（约45°），两脚全脚掌着地，上体正对前方；目视前方。（图2-8）

要点：挺胸、立腰、沉髋，前脚与后脚跟内侧呈一条直线。

Stand with your feet together, and put both fists on the waist, with the center of the fists facing upward; take a step forward with your left (right) foot (4 to 5 times the length of your own foot), bend your knees and squat, with your thigh in a horizontal position, and toes slightly turning inwards; the knee doesn't go over the toes; the right (left) leg stays straight, with the toes turning obliquely forward (about 45°); the soles of both feet are on the ground, and the upper body is facing the front; look ahead. (Fig. 2-8)

Key Points: Keep your chest out, waist up, and hips down, with your front foot and the inside of your back heel in a straight line.

图 2-8　弓步
Fig. 2-8 Bow Stance

3. 仆步 {#section} Drop Stance

两脚平行开立（约本人脚长的4倍），左（右）腿屈膝全蹲，大腿和小腿靠紧，臀部接近小腿，脚尖和膝关节稍外展；右（左）腿挺膝伸直平仆，接近地面，脚尖内扣；两脚全脚掌着地；两手握拳分别抱于腰侧。（图2-9）

要点：挺胸、立腰、沉髋。

Stand with your feet parallel and apart (about 4 times the length of your foot), and squat with your left (right) knee bent, with your thigh and lower leg staying close, hips close to the lower leg, and toes and knee slightly turning outward; your right (left) leg is straight and knee extended straight, close to the ground, with the toes turning inward; the soles of both feet are on the ground; both fists are clenched and put on the waist respectively. (Fig. 2-9)

Key Points: Keep your chest out, waist up, and hips down.

图 2-9　仆步
Fig. 2-9 Drop Stance

4. 歇步 Resting Stance

两腿交叉全蹲，左（右）脚全脚掌着地，脚尖外展；右（左）脚前脚掌着地，膝部贴近左（右）膝外侧，臀部坐于右（左）腿且接近右（左）脚跟处；两手握拳分别抱于腰侧。（图2-10）

要点：挺胸、立腰，两腿靠拢贴紧。

Fully squat with legs crossed, with the left (right) foot on the ground and toes turning outward; keep the front part of the right (left) foot on the ground, the knee close to the outside of the left (right) knee, and the hips on the right leg and close to the right heel; both fists are clenched and put on your waist. (Fig. 2-10)

Key Points: Keep your chest out, waist up, and legs close together.

图 2-10　歇步
Fig. 2-10 Resting Stance

5. 虚步   Cat Stance

两脚前后开立，右（左）脚外展45°，屈膝半蹲，大腿接近水平位；左（右）脚跟离地，脚面绷平，脚尖稍内扣并虚点地面，膝微屈，重心落于右（左）腿。（图2-11）

要点：挺胸、立腰，两腿虚实分明。

Stand with one foot forward and the other backward, with the right (left) foot turning outward by 45°; bend the knees and squat, with both thighs close to the horizontal position; the left (right) heel is off the ground, the soles of the feet are flat, and the toes are slightly turning inward and touching the ground lightly; bend the knees slightly, with the center of gravity falling on the right (left) leg. (Fig. 2-11)

Key Points: Keep your chest out, waist up, and legs in a proper empty position.

图 2-11　虚步
Fig. 2-11 Cat Stance

6. 丁步 T-Stance

　　两腿并拢，一腿全脚掌着地支撑，另一腿与支撑腿内侧相靠，脚尖点地。（图2-12）

　　要点：挺胸、立腰，两腿虚实分明。

Legs stay together, with one leg supported on the ground with the entire sole of the foot, and the other leg resting on the inside of the supporting leg, with the toes on the ground. (Fig. 2-12)

Key Points: Keep your chest out, waist up, and legs in a proper empty position.

图 2-12　丁步
Fig. 2-12 T-Stance

7. 后插步 Rear Cross Stance

左（右）脚抬起，经过右（左）脚后方落步在身体的右（左）侧，左（右）脚前脚掌着地。（图2-13）

要点： 挺胸、立腰、身体中正。

Lift your right (left) foot to pass behind the left (right) foot and land on the left (right) side of the body; the front part of your right (left) sole touches the ground. (Fig. 2-13)

Key Points: Keep your chest out, waist up, and body upright.

图 2-13　后插步
Fig. 2-13 Rear Cross Stance

8. 丁字步 · T-Stance

两脚并步站立，两腿紧靠；一脚尖正对前方，另一脚尖正对侧方，脚跟靠于另一脚的1/2处，两脚成"丁"字形；上体挺胸立腰，身形挺拔（图2-14）。左脚尖对侧方者，称"左丁字步"；右脚尖对侧方者，称"右丁字步"。

要点：收腹、立腰、提臀，两腿间无缝隙。

Stand with feet together, with legs staying close together; one foot faces the front, and the other faces the side, with the heel resting on the middle of the other foot, and the feet forming a "T" shape; keep the upper body straight, chest out and waist up (Fig. 2-14). Those whose left toes face the side are doing the "left T-Stance"; those whose right toes face the side are doing the "right T-Stance".

Key Points: Keep your abdomen in, waist straight, and hips up; no gap between the legs.

图 2-14　丁字步
Fig. 2-14 T-Stance

五、基本腿法　　　　　　　　　　　　Basic Leg Techniques

　　两腿并立，两手握拳分别抱于腰侧；一腿直立作为支撑腿，另一腿由屈到伸向前蹬出，大腿与小腿呈一条直线，高与腰齐，脚尖勾起，力达脚跟。（图2-15）

　　要点：挺胸、直腰、勾脚尖、收髋，蹬腿有寸劲，力达脚跟。

Stand with your legs together, with both fists clenched at the sides of the waist; one leg remains upright for support, and the other leg is kicked forward from flexion to extension, with its thigh and calf in a straight line; the thigh is at the waist level, the toes turn inward, and the force reaches the heel. (Fig. 2-15)

Key Points: Keep your chest out, waist up, toes hooked, and hips closed; kick your leg without brute strength, and the strength reaches your heel.

图 2-15　蹬腿
Fig. 2-15　Kick a Leg

六、平 衡 Balance

提膝平衡 Balance with a Raised Knee

并步站立。一腿直立作为支撑腿，另一腿屈膝高提近胸，脚面绷直，斜垂扣于支撑腿前侧。（图2-16）

要点：站稳，提膝要过腰，提膝腿脚内扣。

Stand with feet together. Stand upright with one leg as the supporting leg, bend the knee of the other leg and raise it close to the chest; keep the sole of the raised foot straight, and the foot slanted over the front of the supporting leg. (Fig. 2-16)

Key Points: To balance, stand firm, raise your knee above your waist, and turn the raised leg and foot inwards.

图 2-16 提膝平衡
Fig. 2-16 Balance with a Raised Knee

刀术动作技法

Broadsword Techniques

一、缠头刀　　　　　　　　　　　　Broadsword Coiling

右手持刀于体侧，刀尖向前，左手向前推出呈立掌；右臂内旋上举，刀尖下垂，左臂屈肘，左掌至右上臂外侧，呈立掌；刀背沿左肩贴背绕过右肩，向左平扫至左肋，刀刃向外，刀尖向后，左掌掌心向上架于头顶上方。（图3-1）

要点：肩要松沉，以腕的转动引导肘关节上提，使刀背贴靠肩背，同时左手须协调配合。

Use your right hand to hold the broadsword to the side of your body, with the tip of the broadsword pointing forward, and your left palm pushed forward to form a standing palm; the right arm is rotated inward and raised, with the tip of the broadsword drooping, the left arm bent, and the left palm extended to the outside of the right upper arm, forming a standing palm; keep the spine of the broadsword close to your back, coil it round from the left shoulder to the right, sweep it to the left to the left rib, with the blade facing outward, the tip of the blade facing backward, and your left palm placed above your head. (Fig. 3-1)

Key Points: Keep your shoulders loose, turn the wrist to lift the elbow up, so that the spine of the broadsword stays close to the back and shoulders; the left hand must be coordinated.

图 3-1　缠头刀
Fig. 3-1 Broadsword Coiling

二、裹脑刀   Broadsword Wrapping

右手握刀于左腋下，刀刃斜向后，刀尖向后上方，右手刀向右平扫，顺势臂外旋屈肘上提，使刀尖下垂；左掌向左下落至平举再屈肘平摆至右腋下，刀背向身后经右肩向左肩外侧绕行；右手持刀下落，置于身体右侧，刀尖向左前方，左手向前推出呈立掌。（图3-2）

要点：肩要松沉，以腕的转动引导肘关节上提，使刀背贴靠肩背，同时左手须协调配合。

Use your right hand to hold the broadsword under the left armpit, with the blade obliquely facing backward, and the tip of the broadsword facing backward and upward; sweep the broadsword to the right, turn your right arm outward and lift the elbow up, with the tip of the blade drooping; lower your left palm to the left until it is in a horizontal position, and then bend the elbow and move it horizontally to under the right armpit; the spine of the broadsword goes behind the back through the right shoulder to the outside of the left shoulder; the broadsword goes down with your right hand, and is placed on the right side of the body, with the tip of the broadsword facing forward to the left, and your left hand pushed forward to form a standing palm. (Fig. 3-2)

Key Points: Keep your shoulders loose, turn the wrist to lift the elbow up, so that the spine of the broadsword stays close to the back and shoulders; the left hand must be coordinated.

图 3-2　裹脑刀
Fig. 3-2　Broadsword Wrapping

三、劈 刀　　　　　　　Broadsword Chopping

右手握刀上举，刀刃向上，刀尖向左，左手按于左胯旁；右手握刀向下劈，力达刀刃，右臂与刀呈一条直线，与肩同高，左臂屈肘，左手立掌于右胸前。（图3-3）

要点：配合腰部用力，眼睛随着刀移动，力达刀刃。

Hold the broadsword with your right hand and lift it up, with the blade facing upward, the tip of the broadsword facing backward, and your left hand pressed against the left hip. Wield the broadsword downwards, with the force reaching the blade; your right arm is in a straight line with the broadsword at the shoulder level, and your left elbow is bent with a standing palm in front of your right chest. (Fig. 3-3)

Key Points: Use your waist to generate force; eyes move with the broadsword, and the force reaches the blade.

图 3-3　劈刀
Fig. 3-3 Broadsword Chopping

四、砍 刀　　　　　　　　　　　Broadsword Cutting

右手持刀，直臂举于右肩斜上方，左掌按于左胯旁；刀向左下方斜砍，力达刀刃前部，同时左掌上合，立掌于右肩前。（图3-4）

要点： 持刀上举时刀尖稍翘起，以刀根部带动刀身向左下方或右下方斜砍。

Hold the broadsword in your right hand, straighten your arm and raise the broadsword diagonally above the right shoulder, press your left palm on the left hip, and wield the broadsword diagonally to the lower left, with the force reaching the front of the blade, and the left palm standing in front of the right shoulder. (Fig. 3-4)

Key Points: When lifting the broadsword up, the tip of it is slightly raised; use the tilt of the broadsword to drive the blade to cut diagonally to the lower left or lower right.

图 3-4　砍刀
Fig. 3-4 Broadsword Cutting

五、截 刀　　　　　　　　　Broadsword Slashing

　　错步站立，右手持刀，直臂前举，左掌立于右肩前；身体右转，左脚收至右脚内侧成丁步，刀刃随转体斜向下截至身体右侧，同时左臂直臂向左斜上方分掌，掌心向前（图3-5）。上截刀刃斜向上，下截刀刃斜向下。

　　要点：以短促的爆发力使刀向斜下猛击，力达刀刃前部。

Stand in a staggered stance, hold the broadsword in your right hand, and straighten and raise your arm forward, with the left palm standing in front of the right shoulder; turn your body to the right, retract the left foot to the inside of the right foot to stand in a T-Stance, and as you turn the body, the blade goes down obliquely to the right side of the body, and the left palm and arm are straightened to the upper left, with the palm facing forwards (Fig. 3-5). To slash upward, the blade is inclined upwards; to slash downwards, the blade is inclined downwards.

Key Points: Strike the broadsword diagonally down with explosive force, which reaches the front of the blade.

图 3-5　截刀
Fig. 3-5 Broadsword Slashing

六、撩　刀　　　　　　　　Broadsword Upper-cutting

　　右手持刀，直臂侧举，左掌立于右肩前，左臂内旋；右臂直臂向上立绕至体后再变外旋，向下沿身体右侧贴身弧形向前撩至体前上方，刀刃向上，力达刀刃前部（图3-6）。正撩时前臂外旋，刀沿身体右侧贴身弧形撩出，手心向上；反撩时前臂内旋，刀沿身体左侧贴身弧形撩出，虎口向下。

　　要点：撩刀时手腕要松活，以腰带臂，用力较柔和，力达刀刃前部。

Hold the broadsword in your right hand and straighten and raise your arm sideways; the left palm stands in front of your right shoulder, with the arm turning inward; keep your right arm straight and up, circle it round to the back of the body, then turns it outward, and wields it downward along the right side of the body and do the upper-cutting in an arc to the top front of the body, with the blade facing up, and the force reaching the front of the blade (Fig. 3-6). When upper-cutting forward, turn your forearm outward, wield the broadsword in an arc along the right side of the body, and your palm faces upward; when upper-cutting in reverse, turn your forearm inward, wield the broadsword in an arc along the left side of the body, and the part between your thumb and index finger faces downward.

Key Points: When upper-cutting, loosen your wrist, and use your waist to drive your arm; exert force gently, and the force reaches the front of the blade.

图 3-6　撩刀
Fig. 3-6 Broadsword Upper-cutting

七、挂 刀   Broadsword Hanging

　　右手持刀，两臂侧平举；右臂内旋，扣腕，刀尖向下；右手刀向左贴身挂出，两手合于腹前（图3-7）。向右为右挂刀，向上为上挂刀，贴身立圆挂一周为抢挂刀。

　　要点：转腰、扣腕，左挂刀满把握住刀柄，右挂刀用拇指与食指刁握刀柄，腕部放松，力达刀背前部。

Hold the broadsword in your right hand and raise your arms sideways. Turn your right arm inward and bend the wrist, point the broadsword downwards, wield it to the left, and place both hands in front of the abdomen (Fig. 3-7). One can hang the broadsword to the right, or hang it upward. If the broadsword goes in a vertical circle around the body, it is called broadsword swinging and hanging.

Key Points: Turn your waist and bend the wrist. To hang the broadsword to the left, you should fully grip the broadsword handle; to hang the broadsword to the right, you should use the thumb and index finger to hold the handle, relax the wrist, and the force reaches the front of the broadsword spine.

图 3-7　挂刀
Fig. 3-7　Broadsword Hanging

八、扎 刀 Broadsword Thrusting

右手持刀于身体右侧，刀尖向前，左掌按于左胯旁；右臂屈肘上提再直臂向前直刺，左掌弧形上摆，立于右前臂内侧（图3-8）。根据扎的高度，扎刀分为上扎刀、平扎刀、下扎刀。

要点：快速发力，扎刀力达刀尖，刀与右臂呈一条直线。

Use your right hand to hold the broadsword to the right side of the body, point the broadsword forward, and put the left palm next to the left hip; bend and raise the right elbow and then straighten your arm to thrust the broadsword forward, and swing the left palm upward in an arc to form a standing palm on the inside of the right forearm (Fig. 3-8). Depending on the height of the thrust, broadsword thrusting could be upper thrusting, horizontal thrusting or downward thrusting.

Key Points: Exert force swiftly, with the force reaching the tip of the broadsword, and the broadsword and right arm in a straight line.

图 3-8　扎刀
Fig. 3-8 Broadsword Thrusting

九、斩 刀 Broadsword Hacking

右手持刀，直臂前举，左掌立于右上臂内侧；身体右转，右臂内旋，刀向右横击，同时左臂直臂向左侧平分。（图3-9）

要点： 以腰拧转助力，力达刀刃。

Hold the broadsword in your right hand, and straighten and raise the arm forward, with the left palm standing on the inside of the right upper arm. Turn your body to the right, turn the right arm inward, and strike the broadsword horizontally to the right, while swinging the left arm to the upper left. (Fig. 3-9)

Key Points: Turn your waist to help exert force, which reaches the blade.

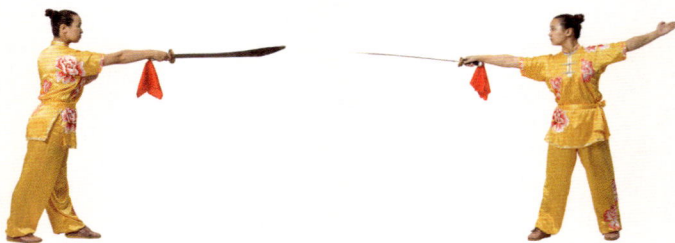

图 3-9　斩刀
Fig. 3-9 Broadsword Hacking

十、扫 刀 　　　　　　　　　Broadsword Sweeping

左脚在后下蹲成歇步，右手持刀于身体右侧，刀尖与踝关节同高，左掌举于左斜上方；身体左转约270°，右臂外旋，刀刃向左，随转体向左旋转平扫一周，左掌合按于右手腕处。（图3-10）

要点：刀身要平，刀刃向左（或右），身体重心在两脚之间，扫刀速度要快，力达刀刃。

Squat down with the left foot in the back to be in a resting stance; use your right hand to hold the broadsword with a straight arm to the right side of your body, with the tip of the broadsword at the same height as the ankle; raise the left palm with a straight arm inclined to the left, turn your body by about 270° to the left, and turn the right arm outward. Turn the blade to the left, and as the body turns, sweep the broadsword to the left in a circle, and press the left palm against the right wrist. (Fig. 3-10)

Key Points: Keep the blade flat, and the blade should point to the left (or right); the center of gravity of the body should be between your feet, and the sweeping should be swift enough to enable the force to reach the blade.

图 3-10　扫刀
Fig. 3-10 Broadsword Sweeping

十一、挑 刀   Broadsword Upward Slitting

右手持刀，直臂侧平举，左掌立于右上臂内侧；右臂直臂上挑，左掌立于右肩前。（图3-11）

要点：右手握住刀柄，虎口向上；向上挑刀，右臂伸直与刀呈一条直线，力达刀尖或刀背前段。

Hold the broadsword in your right hand and straighten and raise the right arm to a horizontal position, with the left palm standing on the inner side of the right upper arm; the right arm is lifted straight upward, with the left palm standing in front of the right shoulder. (Fig. 3-11)

Key Points: Grip the broadsword handle with the right hand, with the part between the thumb and index finger facing upward; straighten the right arm and lift it up in a straight line with the broadsword, with the force reaching the tip of the broadsword or the front of the broadsword spine.

图 3-11　挑刀
Fig. 3-11 Broadsword Upward Slitting

十二、按 刀 Broadsword Pressing

右手持刀侧平举，左臂侧平举；右臂外旋，刀向上弧形按于身体左侧，与腰同高，刀尖向左，左掌合按于右手腕处，目视刀尖（图3-12）。刀与腰平为平按刀，接近地面为低按刀。

要点：左手附于右手腕或刀背处以助力。

Hold the broadsword in your right hand and raise it sideways to a horizontal position; straighten the left arm and raise the left palm sideways horizontally; turn your right arm inward and wield the broadsword upward in an arc and press it to the left side of the body at the waist level, with the tip of the broadsword facing the left, the left palm pressed on the right wrist, and eyes on the tip of the broadsword (Fig. 3-12). You can press the broadsword at the waist level or press it close to the ground.

Key Points: Your left hand is attached to the right wrist or the spine of the blade.

图 3-12　按刀
Fig. 3-12 Broadsword Pressing

十三、藏 刀　　　　Broadsword Concealing

右手持刀，刀身横平（刀尖向后，刀刃向外）藏于左腰后为拦腰藏刀；刀身竖直藏于左臂后为立藏刀（刀尖向上，刀刃向外）；刀尖斜向下藏于右髋旁，左掌前推为平藏刀（刀尖向前，刀刃向下）。（图3-13）

要点：注意前臂与刀身动作路线为弧形，目视前方。

Hold the broadsword in your right hand; there are three ways to conceal the broadsword: 1) keep the blade horizontal and flat (with the tip of the blade facing backward, and the edge of the blade facing outward), and conceal the broadsword behind the left waist; 2) keep the blade vertical and conceal the broadsword behind the left arm (with the tip of the blade facing upward, and the edge of the blade facing outward); 3) keep the tip of the blade obliquely downward and conceal the broadsword next to the right hip, and your left palm is pushed forward with a straight arm (with the tip of the broadsword facing forward, and the blade facing downward). (Fig. 3-13)

Key Points: Note that the movement of your forearm and the blade should resemble an arc, and look straight ahead.

图 3-13　藏刀
Fig. 3-13 Broadsword Concealing

十四、推　刀 　　　　　　　　　　　　　Broadsword Pushing

右手持刀于胯旁，刀尖向前，左掌垂直于体侧；右臂内旋，刀尖向下，刀刃向前，屈肘上提再直臂向前立推，左手附于刀背前部（图3–14）。刀刃向前、向左、向右推出为立推刀，刀尖向左为平推刀。

要点：刀身竖直，左手助推刀背。

Use your right hand to hold the broadsword next to the hip, with the tip of the blade pointing forward, and the left palm being perpendicular to the side of the body; turn your right arm inward, the tip of the blade faces downward, and the blade faces forward; bend and raise your elbow, and then straighten and push your arm forward, with your left hand attached to the front of the blade spine (Fig. 3-14). If you push the broadsword forward, to the left or right, it is called vertical broadsword pushing; if the tip of the broadsword faces the left, it is called horizontal broadsword pushing.

Key Points: Keep the blade vertical and use your left hand to help push the spine of the blade.

图 3–14　推刀
Fig. 3-14 Broadsword Pushing

十五、架 刀 Broadsword Supporting

右手持刀，直臂前平举，左掌立于右上臂内侧；右臂屈肘内旋，刀尖摆向左侧，左手附于刀身前部，双手向上横向托刀，刀刃向上，刀高过头。（图3-15）

要点： 刀自下而上架起，刀身保持横平，力点在刀身中部。

Hold the broadsword in your right hand, raise a straight arm forward, and the left palm stands on the inner side of the right forearm; bend your right elbow and turn it inward, with the tip of the broadsword swinging to the left; attach your left hand to the front of the blade and raise your hands, with the broadsword in a horizontal position above your head, and its blade facing up. (Fig. 3-15)

Key Points: The broadsword is raised upward, keep the blade horizontal, and the force falls in the middle of the blade.

图 3-15 架刀
Fig. 3-15 Broadsword Supporting

十六、带 刀　　　　　　　　Broadsword Deflecting

　　右手持刀，直臂前平举，左掌立于右前臂内侧；右臂内旋使刀刃向右，腰向右转，右手随腰由前向右侧回抽，左掌附于右手腕处（图3-16）。带刀属于防守型刀法，意在用己兵刃牵引对方器械，使之偏离进攻目标，运动轨迹接近于直线。

　　要点：以腰带臂，以臂带刀，力点由刀身根部前移。

Hold the broadsword in your right hand, raise a straight arm forward, and your left palm stands on the inside of the right forearm. Turn your arm inward to make the blade face the right, and turn your waist to the right, with your right hand drawn back from the front to the right, and the left palm attached to the right wrist (Fig. 3-16). Broadsword deflecting is a defense technique, which is to use your own broadsword to lead the opponent's weapon, so that it deviates from the attacking target; the movement of the broadsword resembles a straight line.

Key Points: Use your waist to drive your arm to lead the broadsword, and the force moves forward from the base of the broadsword.

图 3-16　带刀
Fig. 3-16 Broadsword Deflecting

十七、抹 刀　　　　　Broadsword Smearing

右手持刀，直臂前平举，左掌立于右前臂内侧；腰向右拧转，右臂内旋，刀刃向外，由前向右弧形抽回；左掌顺势助力，仍按于右前臂内侧（图3-17）。抹刀属于进攻型刀法，高度在胸部以上，运动轨迹接近于弧形。

要点：注意前臂与刀身动作路线为弧形。刀速均匀，用力轻柔，力达刀刃。

Hold the broadsword in your right hand, raise a straight arm forward, and your left palm stands on the inner side of the right forearm; turn your waist to the right, and turn your right arm inward, with the edge of the blade facing the right and drawn back in an arc from the front to the right, which is called "mo dao" in Chinese. Use your left palm to help exert force, but it remains pressed on the inside of your right forearm (Fig. 3-17). Broadsword smearing is an attacking technique and should be above the chest, the broadsword flows in the shape of an arc.

Key Points: Note that the forearm and blade move in the shape of an arc. Keep the speed consistent; the force is gentle and reaches the edge of the blade.

图 3-17　抹刀
Fig. 3-17 Broadsword Smearing

十八、撩腕花　　　　Broadsword Spinning

以腕为轴，刀在身体两侧由后向前上贴身立圆绕环，刃背分明。（图3-18）

要点：手臂保持不动，手腕放松，刀花呈立圆。

With the wrist as the axis, the broadsword stands on both sides of the body from the back to the front, and surrounds the body in a circle; the edge and spine of the broadsword are distinct. (Fig. 3-18)

Key Points: Your arm remains still, relax your wrist, and spin the broadsword in a vertical circle.

图 3-18　撩腕花
Fig. 3-18 Broadsword Spinning

十九、点 刀 　　　　　Broadsword Downward Poking

右手持刀，直臂侧平举，左臂侧平举；右手提腕，刀尖猛向下点，左掌合按于右手腕处。（图3-19）

要点：手腕放松，突然而短促地用力上提，使刀尖向下啄击，力达刀尖。

Hold the broadsword in your right hand, raise the arm straight to the side, and raise your left palm straight to the side; raise your right wrist, point the tip of the blade downward abruptly and press your left palm on the right wrist. (Fig. 3-19)

Key Points: Relax your wrist, and lift it up abruptly, so that the tip of the blade pokes down, and the force reaches the tip of the blade.

图 3-19　点刀
Fig. 3-19 Broadsword Downward Poking

二十、崩 刀　　　　Broadsword Upward Poking

右手持刀，直臂侧平举，左臂侧平举；右手沉腕，使刀尖猛向上崩，左掌内合按于右前臂内侧。（图3-20）

要点： 手腕突然用力下沉，使刀尖由下向上啄击，力达刀尖。

Hold the broadsword in your right hand, raise the arm straight to the side, and raise the left palm straight to the side. Lower your right wrist, so that the tip of the blade pokes upward, and press your left palm on the inside of your right forearm. (Fig. 3-20)

Key Points: Lower your wrist suddenly with force, leading the tip of the broadsword to poke from the bottom up, with the force reaching the tip of the broadsword.

图 3-20　崩刀
Fig. 3-20 Broadsword Upward Poking

二十一、格 刀　　　　　　　　Broadsword Blocking

右手持刀，直臂前平举，左掌立于右前臂内侧；右臂内旋，刀尖向下，刀刃向外；身体右转，右手持刀向右格挡，左掌仍按于右前臂内侧。（图3-21）

要点： 刀身竖直，以腰带动手臂和手腕用力。

Hold the broadsword in your right hand, raise the arm straight and forward, and the left palm stands on the inside of your right forearm; turn your right arm inward, with the tip of the blade facing downward, and the blade facing outward; turn your body to the right, hold the broadsword in your right hand to block to the right, and the left palm remains pressed against the inside of your right forearm. (Fig. 3-21)

Key Points: Keep the blade vertical, and use your waist to drive your arm and wrist to exert force.

图 3-21　格刀
Fig. 3-21　Broadsword Blocking

刀术段前九级考评技术内容

A Nine-tier Pre-Duan Grading System for Broadsword Play

刀术段前一级　　Broadsword Play: Pre-Duan Level 1

刀术段前一级
Broadsword Play:
Pre-Duan Level 1

技术内容：刀法＋手型

（1）招数：1 个动作。

（2）技法：2 种（缠头、裹脑）。

（3）手型：1 种（掌）。

Technical Content: Broadsword Technique ＋ Hand Form

(1) Move: 1 move.

(2) Technique: 2 techniques (broadsword coiling, wrapping).

(3) Hand form: 1 hand form (palm).

练习刀术段前一级开始前行抱刀礼。

Before your practice, perform the broadsword-holding salute.

1.预备势   Preparatory Posture

要点：挺胸抬头，气息平稳，精神饱满，目视前方。（图4-1）

Key Points: Keep your chest up and breathe steadily; stay energetic and look straight ahead. (Fig. 4-1)

图 4-1 预备势
Fig. 4-1 Preparatory Posture

2.缠头裹脑　　　　　　　　　　　　　　Broadsword Coiling and Wrapping

要点：腕部发力使得刀背贴身，目视前方，动作协调连贯。（图4-2）

Key Points: Use your wrist to exert force so that the spine of the blade is close to the body; look straight ahead; keep the movements coordinated and coherent. (Fig. 4-2)

图 4-2　缠头裹脑
Fig. 4-2 Broadsword Coiling and Wrapping

练习刀术段前一级结束后行抱刀礼。

At the end of your practice, perform the broadsword-holding salute.

刀术段前二级　　Broadsword Play: Pre-Duan Level 2

刀术段前二级
Broadsword Play:
Pre-Duan Level 2

技术内容：刀法＋步型＋手型

（1）招数：1 个动作。

（2）技法：2 种（劈刀、扎刀）。

（3）步型：1 种（弓步）。

（4）手型：1 种（掌）。

Technical Content: Broadsword Technique ＋ Stance ＋ Hand Form

(1) Move: 1 move.

(2) Technique: 2 techniques (broadsword chopping, thrusting).

(3) Stance: 1 stance (bow stance).

(4) Hand form: 1 hand form (palm).

练习刀术段前二级开始前行抱刀礼。

Before your practice, perform the broadsword-holding salute.

1.预备势   Preparatory Posture

要点：挺胸抬头，气息平稳，精神饱满，目视前方。（图4-3）

Key Points: Keep your chest up and breathe steadily; stay energetic and look straight ahead. (Fig. 4-3)

图 4-3　预备势
Fig. 4-3 Preparatory Posture

2. 弓步劈扎刀   Broadsword Chopping and Thrusting in a Bow Stance

要点：右手握刀自上而右劈刀，随后刀从腰间扎出，扎刀迅速，劲力顺达，力达刀尖，动作协调连贯。（图4-4）

Key Points: Hold the broadsword in your right hand and chop with it from top to right, and then thrust with it swiftly from the waist, with the force reaching the tip of the blade; keep the movements coordinated and coherent. (Fig. 4-4)

图 4-4　弓步劈扎刀

Fig. 4-4 Broadsword Chopping and Thrusting in a Bow Stance

练习刀术段前二级结束后行抱刀礼。

At the end of your practice, perform the broadsword-holding salute.

刀术段前三级　　Broadsword Play: Pre-Duan Level 3

刀术段前三级
Broadsword Play:
Pre-Duan Level 3

技术内容：刀法＋步型＋手型

（1）招数：3 个动作。

（2）技法：3 种（挂刀、撩刀、斩刀）。

（3）步型：1 种（弓步）。

（4）手型：1 种（掌）。

Technical Content: Broadsword Technique ＋ Stance ＋ Hand Form

(1) Move: 3 moves.

(2) Technique: 3 techniques (broadsword hanging, upper-cutting, hacking).

(3) Stance: 1 stance (bow stance).

(4) Hand form: 1 hand form (palm).

练习刀术段前三级开始前行抱刀礼。

Before your practice, perform the broadsword-holding salute.

1. 预备势 Preparatory Posture

要点： 挺胸抬头，气息平稳，精神饱满，目视前方。（图4-5）

Key Points: Keep your chest up and breathe steadily; stay energetic and look straight ahead. (Fig. 4-5)

图 4-5　预备势
Fig. 4-5 Preparatory Posture

2. 上步挂刀 　　　　　　　　　Broadsword Hanging After Stepping Forward

要点：力达刀背前部，挂刀贴身，腕部放松，动作协调连贯。（图4-6）

Key Points: The force reaches the front of the broadsword spine; hang the broadsword close to the body, relax your wrist, and keep the movements coordinated and coherent. (Fig. 4-6)

图 4-6　上步挂刀

Fig. 4-6 Broadsword Hanging After Stepping Forward

3. 转身撩刀 　　　　　　　　　Broadsword Upper-cutting While Turning the Body

要点：贴身撩刀，刀走立圆，力达刀刃。（图4-7）

Key Points: Keep the broadsword close to the body when upper-cutting; the broadsword moves in a vertical circle, and the force reaches the blade. (Fig. 4-7)

图 4-7　转身撩刀

Fig. 4-7 Broadsword Upper-cutting While Turning the Body

4. 弓步斩刀　　　　　　　Broadsword Hacking in a Bow Stance

要点：动作协调连贯，平斩力达刀刃前部。（图4-8）

Key Points: Keep the movements coordinated and coherent; the cutting force reaches the front of the blade. (Fig. 4-8)

图 4-8　弓步斩刀
Fig. 4-8 Broadsword Hacking in a Bow Stance

练习刀术段前三级结束后行抱刀礼。

At the end of your practice, perform the broadsword-holding salute.

刀术段前四级　　Broadsword Play: Pre-Duan Level 4

刀术段前四级
Broadsword Play:
Pre-Duan Level 4

技术内容：刀法＋步型＋手型

（1）招数：3 个动作。

（2）技法：4 种（点刀、崩刀、藏刀、斩刀）。

（3）步型：2 种（弓步、马步）。

（4）手型：1 种（掌）。

Technical Content: Broadsword Technique ＋ Stance ＋ Hand Form

(1) Move: 3 moves.

(2)Technique: 4 techniques (broadsword downward poking, upward poking, concealing, hacking).

(3) Stance: 2 stances (bow stance, horse stance).

(4) Hand form: 1 hand form (palm).

练习刀术段前四级开始前行抱刀礼。

Before your practice, perform the broadsword-holding salute.

1. 预备势   Preparatory Posture

要点：挺胸抬头，气息平稳，精神饱满，目视前方。（图4-9）

Key Points: Keep your chest up and breathe steadily; stay energetic and look straight ahead. (Fig. 4-9)

图 4-9　预备势
Fig. 4-9 Preparatory Posture

2. 弓步点崩刀   Downward and Upward Poking in a Bow Stance

要点：屈腕充分，手腕发力，力达刀尖，点崩连贯。（图4-10）

Key Points: Bend your wrist fully and use it to exert force, which reaches the tip of the blade; keep the poking points coherent. (Fig. 4-10)

图 4-10　弓步点崩刀
Fig. 4-10 Downward and Upward Poking in a Bow Stance

3. 马步藏刀　　　　　　　　　　Broadsword Concealing in a Horse Stance

要点：步型稳健，以腰拧转助力，动作协调连贯。（图4-11）

Key Points: Maintain a steady horse stance and turn your waist to exert force; keep the movements coordinated and coherent. (Fig. 4-11)

图 4-11　马步藏刀
Fig. 4-11 Broadsword Concealing in a Horse Stance

4. 弓步斩刀　　　　　　　　　　Broadsword Hacking in a Bow Stance

要点：步型变换迅速稳健，力达刀刃，动作连贯。（图4-12）

Key Points: Change your stance fast and steadily; the force reaches the blade; keep the movements coherent. (Fig. 4-12)

图 4-12　弓步斩刀
Fig. 4-12 Broadsword Hacking in a Bow Stance

练习刀术段前四级结束后行抱刀礼。

At the end of your practice, perform the broadsword-holding salute.

刀术段前五级　　　Broadsword Play: Pre-Duan Level 5

刀术段前五级
Broadsword Play:
Pre-Duan Level 5

技术内容：刀法＋步型＋手型

（1）招数：5 个动作。

（2）技法：6 种（扎刀、挂刀、劈刀、缠头、裹脑、斩刀）。

（3）步型：2 种（马步、弓步）。

（4）手型：1 种（掌）。

Technical Content: Broadsword Technique ＋ Stance ＋ Hand Form

(1) Move: 5 moves.

(2) Technique: 6 techniques (broadsword thrusting, hanging, chopping, coiling, wrapping, hacking).

(3) Stance: 2 stances (horse stance, bow stance).

(4) Hand form: 1 hand form (palm).

练习刀术段前五级开始前行抱刀礼。

Before your practice, perform the broadsword-holding salute.

1. 预备势 Preparatory Posture

要点： 挺胸抬头，气息平稳，精神饱满，目视前方。（图4-13）

Key Points: Keep your chest up and breathe steadily; stay energetic and look straight ahead. (Fig. 4-13)

图 4-13　预备势
Fig. 4-13 Preparatory Posture

2. 弓步扎刀 Broadsword Thrusting in a Bow Stance

要点： 劲力顺达，以腰带力，力达刀尖。（图4-14）

Key Points: Keep the strength and force flowing, and use your waist to lead the broadsword, with the force reaching the tip of the blade. (Fig. 4-14)

图 4-14　弓步扎刀
Fig. 4-14 Broadsword Thrusting in a Bow Stance

3. 上步挂刀　　　　　Broadsword Hanging After Stepping Forward

要点：动作协调，挂刀扣腕，腕部放松，力达刀背前部。（图4-15）

Key Points: Coordinate the movements, hang the broadsword and press your palm against the wrist; relax the wrist; the force reaches the front of the broadsword spine. (Fig. 4-15)

图 4-15　上步挂刀
Fig. 4-15　Broadsword Hanging After Stepping Forward

4. 并步劈刀　　　　　Broadsword Chopping with Feet Together

要点：刀贴身，画立圆，腕部发力，力达刀尖。（图4-16）

Key Points: Keep the broadsword close to the body, and draw a vertical circle; use the wrist to exert force, which reaches the tip of the blade. (Fig. 4-16)

图 4-16　并步劈刀
Fig. 4-16　Broadsword Chopping with Feet Together

5. 马步缠头裹脑刀　　　　　　Broadsword Coiling and Wrapping in a Horse Stance

要点： 肩要松沉，以腕的转动引导肘关节上提，刀背贴身，动作连贯。（图4-17）

Key Points: Relax your shoulders; turn your wrist to lead the elbow to lift up; keep the spine of the blade close to the body, and the movements coherent. (Fig. 4-17)

图 4-17　马步缠头裹脑刀
Fig. 4-17 Broadsword Coiling and Wrapping in a Horse Stance

6. 并步斩刀　　　　　　　　　Broadsword Hacking with Feet Together

要点： 重心稳定，腰腕发力，力达刀刃。（图4-18）

Key Points: Keep your center of gravity stable, and use your waist and wrist to exert force, which reaches the blade. (Fig. 4-18)

图 4-18　并步斩刀
Fig. 4-18 Broadsword Hacking with Feet Together

练习刀术段前五级结束后行抱刀礼。

At the end of your practice, perform the broadsword-holding salute.

刀术段前六级　　　Broadsword Play: Pre-Duan Level 6

刀术段前六级
Broadsword Play:
Pre-Duan Level 6

技术内容：刀法＋步型＋手型

（1）招数：5 个动作。

（2）技法：6 种（缠头、扫刀、裹脑、截刀、推刀、藏刀）。

（3）步型：3 种（弓步、歇步、虚步）。

（4）手型：1 种（掌）。

Technical Content: Broadsword Technique ＋ Stance ＋ Hand Form

(1) Move: 5 moves.

(2) Technique: 6 techniques (broadsword coiling, sweeping, wrapping, slashing, pushing, concealing).

(3) Stance: 3 stances (bow stance, resting stance, cat stance).

(4) Hand form: 1 hand form (palm).

练习刀术段前六级开始前行抱刀礼。

Before your practice, perform the broadsword-holding salute.

1. 预备势　　　　　　　　　　　　　　　　　　Preparatory Posture

要点： 挺胸抬头，气息平稳，精神饱满，目视前方。（图4-19）

Key Points: Keep your chest up and breathe steadily; stay energetic and look straight ahead. (Fig. 4-19)

图 4-19　预备势
Fig. 4-19 Preparatory Posture

2. 缠头扫刀　　　　　　　　　　　　Broadsword Coiling and Sweeping

要点： 刀背贴身，起落协调，落步稳健，身械配合，衔接过程流畅。（图4-20）

Key Points: Keep the broadsword spine close to the body, and coordinate the rise and fall of the broadsword; remain steady, and coordinate the body and broadsword to keep the movements flowing. (Fig. 4-20)

图 4-20　缠头扫刀

Fig. 4-20 Broadsword Coiling and Sweeping

3. 裹脑歇步截刀　Broadsword Wrapping Followed by Slashing in a Resting Stance

要点：裹脑肢体与步法协调，截刀有力度，力达刀刃，动作连贯，一气呵成。（图4-21）

Key Points: When performing the wrapping, coordinate your limbs and footwork; the slashing should be powerful, with the force reaching the blade; keep the movements coherent without interruption. (Fig. 4-21)

图 4-21　裹脑歇步截刀

Fig. 4-21 Broadsword Wrapping Followed by Slashing in a Resting Stance

4. 弓步推刀　　　　　　　　　　　Broadsword Pushing in a Bow Stance

要点：刀贴于身，走立圆，推刀有爆发力，力达刀刃。（图4-22）

Key Points: Keep the broadsword close to the body, and wield it in a vertical circle; push the broadsword with explosive force, which reaches the edge of the blade. (Fig. 4-22)

图 4-22　弓步推刀
Fig. 4-22 Broadsword Pushing in a Bow Stance

5. 弓步藏刀　　　　　　　　　　　Broadsword Concealing in a Bow Stance

要点：腕部发力，动作迅速，弓步扎实，力达刀背。（图4-23）

Key Points: Exert force with your waist, and keep the movements swift; maintain a solid bow stance, and the force reaches the blade spine. (Fig. 4-23)

图 4-23　弓步藏刀
Fig. 4-23 Broadsword Concealing in a Bow Stance

6. 虚步藏刀　　　　　　　　　Broadsword Concealing in a Cat Stance

要点： 重心平稳，持刀手腕内扣，目视前方。（图4-24）

Key Points: Keep your center of gravity stable, turn inward the wrist of the hand holding the broadsword, and look straight ahead. (Fig. 4-24)

图 4-24　虚步藏刀
Fig. 4-24　Broadsword Concealing in a Cat Stance

练习刀术段前六级结束后行抱刀礼。

At the end of your practice, perform the broadsword-holding salute.

刀术段前七级   Broadsword Play: Pre-Duan Level 7

刀术段前七级
Broadsword Play:
Pre-Duan Level 7

技术内容：刀法 + 步型 + 手型 + 腿法

（1）招数：7 个动作。

（2）技法：7 种（扎刀、撩刀、劈刀、挂刀、撩腕花、带刀、按刀）。

（3）步型：2 种（弓步、仆步）。

（4）手型：1 种（掌）。

（5）腿法：1 种（蹬腿）。

Technical Content: Broadsword Technique + Stance + Hand Form + Footwork

(1) Move: 7 moves.

(2) Technique: 7 techniques (broadsword thrusting, upper-cutting, chopping, hanging, spinning, deflecting, pressing).

(3) Stance: 2 stances (bow stance, drop stance).

(4) Hand form: 1 hand form (palm).

(5) Footwork: 1 (kicking).

练习刀术段前七级开始前行抱刀礼。

Before your practice, perform the broadsword-holding salute.

1. 预备势 　　　　　　　　　　　　　　　　　Preparatory Posture

要点： 挺胸抬头，气息平稳，精神饱满，目视前方。（图4-25）

Key Points: Keep your chest up and breathe steadily; stay energetic and look straight ahead. (Fig. 4-25)

图 4-25　预备势
Fig. 4-25 Preparatory Posture

2. 弓步扎刀 　　　　　　　　　　　Broadsword Thrusting in a Bow Stance

要点： 自腰发力，扎刀迅速，力达刀尖，弓步扎实。（图4-26）

Key Points: Exert force from your waist; perform the thrusting swiftly, with the force reaching the tip of the blade; maintain a solid bow stance. (Fig. 4-26)

图 4-26　弓步扎刀
Fig. 4-26 Broadsword Thrusting in a Bow Stance

3. 反撩刀　　　　　　　　　　　　Reverse Broadsword Upper-cutting

要点： 贴身立圆，眼随刀动，力达刀刃，动作连贯。（图4-27）

Key Points: The broadsword stays close to your body and moves in a vertical circle; eyes move with the broadsword, with the force reaching the edge of the blade; keep the movements coherent. (Fig. 4-27)

图 4-27　反撩刀
Fig. 4-27 Reverse Broadsword Upper-cutting

4. 左右抡劈刀　　　　Broadsword Swinging Left and Right Followed by Chopping

要点： 以腰带刀画立圆，抡劈连贯有力，力达刀刃前部，眼随刀动。（图4-28）

Key Points: Use your waist to lead the broadsword to move in a vertical circle, keep the swinging and chopping coherent and powerful, with the force reaching the front of the blade, and eyes move with the broadsword. (Fig. 4-28)

图 4-28　左右抡劈刀
Fig. 4-28 Broadsword Swinging Left and Right Followed by Chopping

5. 上步挂刀　　　　　　　　Broadsword Hanging After Stepping Forward

要点： 转身轻灵，挂刀贴身走立圆，力达刀背前部。（图4-29）

Key Points: Turn around gently; hang the broadsword, which stays close to the body and moves in a vertical circle, with the force reaching the front of the blade spine. (Fig. 4-29)

图 4-29　上步挂刀
Fig. 4-29 Broadsword Hanging After Stepping Forward

6. 弓步扎刀　　　　　　　　Broadsword Thrusting in a Bow Stance

要点： 劲力顺达，扎刀迅猛，力达刀尖，弓步扎实。（图4-30）

Key Points: Keep your strength and force flowing smoothly, and perform the thrusting swiftly, with the force reaching the tip of the blade; maintain a solid bow stance. (Fig. 4-30)

图 4-30　弓步扎刀
Fig. 4-30 Broadsword Thrusting in a Bow Stance

7. 撩腕花蹬腿带刀

Broadsword Spinning and Kicking a Leg for Broadsword Deflecting

要点：撩腕花与蹬腿带刀动作应协调连贯，蹬腿有力，重心稳定。（图4-31）

Key Points: Keep the two moves coordinated and coherent; kick your leg with force, and keep your center of gravity stable. (Fig. 4-31)

图 4-31　撩腕花蹬腿带刀
Fig. 4-31　Broadsword Spinning and Kicking a Leg for Broadsword Deflecting

8. 仆步按刀

Broadsword Pressing in a Drop Stance

要点：步型变换快速稳定，按刀有力，力达刀刃。（图4-32）

Key Points: Change your footwork swiftly and steadily, and press the broadsword with force, which reaches the blade. (Fig. 4-32)

图 4-32　仆步按刀
Fig. 4-32　Broadsword Pressing in a Drop Stance

练习刀术段前七级结束后行抱刀礼。

At the end of your practice, perform the broadsword-holding salute.

刀术段前八级 　　Broadsword Play: Pre-Duan Level 8

刀术段前八级
Broadsword Play:
Pre-Duan Level 8

技术内容：刀法 + 步型 + 手型 + 平衡

（1）招数：10个动作。

（2）技法：9种（藏刀、扎刀、挑刀、砍刀、按刀、架刀、挂刀、劈刀、抹刀）。

（3）步型：4种（虚步、弓步、丁步、马步）。

（4）手型：2种（掌、勾手）。

（5）平衡：1种。

Technical Content: Broadsword Technique + Stance + Hand Form + Balance

(1) Move: 10 moves.

(2) Technique: 9 techniques (broadsword concealing, thrusting, upward slitting, cutting, pressing, supporting, hanging, chopping, smearing).

(3) Stance: 4 stances (cat stance, bow stance, T-Stance, horse stance).

(4) Hand form: 2 hand forms (palm, hook).

(5) Balance: 1 balance.

练习刀术段前八级开始前行抱刀礼。

Before your practice, perform the broadsword-holding salute.

1. 预备势   Preparatory Posture

要点： 挺胸抬头，气息平稳，精神饱满，目视前方。（图4-33）

Key Points: Keep your chest up and breathe steadily; stay energetic and look straight ahead. (Fig. 4-33)

图 4-33　预备势
Fig. 4-33 Preparatory Posture

2. 虚步藏刀   Broadsword Concealing in a Cat Stance

要点： 下蹲、推掌、摆头同时进行，一步到位。（图4-34）

Key Points: Squat, push palms, and swing your head simultaneously and at one go. (Fig. 4-34)

图 4-34　虚步藏刀
Fig. 4-34 Broadsword Concealing in a Cat Stance

3. 弓步扎刀   Broadsword Thrusting in a Bow Stance

要点： 经腰间扎出，动作迅速，劲力顺达，力达刀尖，左为勾手。（图4-35）

Key Points: The broadsword is thrusted from the waist; execute the movement swiftly and keep the force flowing, with the force reaching the tip of the blade; your left hand is hooked. (Fig. 4-35)

图 4-35 弓步扎刀
Fig. 4-35 Broadsword Thrusting in a Bow Stance

4. 并步挑刀   Broadsword Upward Slitting with Feet Together

要点： 挑刀迅速，力达刀背，屈腕，刀尖下垂，左为勾手。（图4-36）

Key Points: Perform the upward slitting swiftly, with the force reaching the broadsword spine; bend your wrist, the tip of the blade hangs down, and your left hand is hooked. (Fig. 4-36)

图 4-36 并步挑刀
Fig. 4-36 Broadsword Upward Slitting with Feet Together

5. 提膝砍刀 Broadsword Cutting with a Knee Up

要点：以腕发力，砍刀迅速，提膝平稳，眼随刀动。（图4-37）

Key Points: Use your wrist to exert force, and make sure the cutting is swift; raise your knee steadily, and eyes move with the broadsword. (Fig. 4-37)

图 4-37　提膝砍刀
Fig. 4-37 Broadsword Cutting with a Knee Up

6. 丁步按刀 Broadsword Pressing in a T-Stance

要点：由裹脑刀接小跳步后做丁步按刀，小跳步注意重心平衡，力达刀刃。（图4-38）

Key Points: Shift from broadsword wrapping to a hop stance, and then press the broadsword in a T-Stance. When in a hop stance, pay attention to the balance of the center of gravity; the force reaches the blade. (Fig. 4-38)

图 4-38　丁步按刀
Fig. 4-38 Broadsword Pressing in a T-Stance

7. 提膝架刀　　　　　　　　　Broadsword Supporting with a Knee Up

要点： 起身迅速，提膝平稳，架刀力达刀身。（图4-39）

Key Points: Get up quickly, raise your knee steadily, and support the broadsword, with the force reaching the blade. (Fig. 4-39)

图 4-39　提膝架刀
Fig. 4-39 Broadsword Supporting with a Knee Up

8. 上步挂刀　　　　　　Broadsword Hanging After Stepping Forward

要点： 上身拧转，持刀扣腕，挂刀力达刀刃前部。（图4-40）

Key Points: Turn your upper body, hold the broadsword with your wrist bent, and hang the broadsword, with the force reaching the front of the blade. (Fig. 4-40)

图 4-40　上步挂刀
Fig. 4-40 Broadsword Hanging After Stepping Forward

9. 马步劈刀   Broadsword Chopping in a Horse Stance

要点：转身、马步、劈刀、甩头同时进行，劈刀力达刀刃中前部。
（图4-41）

Key Points: Turn around, stand in a horse stance, chop with the broadsword, and swing your head simultaneously; the force of chopping reaches the middle and front of the blade. (Fig. 4-41)

图 4-41　马步劈刀
Fig. 4-41 Broadsword Chopping in a Horse Stance

10. 上步抹刀   Stepping Forward for Broadsword Smearing

要点：抹刀以腰为轴，力达刀刃，身械协调。（图4-42）

Key Points: Take your waist as the axis for broadsword smearing, with the force reaching the blade; coordinate your body and the weapon. (Fig. 4-42)

图 4-42　上步抹刀
Fig. 4-42 Stepping Forward for Broadsword Smearing

11. 弓步扎刀　　　　　　　　Broadsword Thrusting in a Bow Stance

要点：刀自腰间扎出，快速有力，劲力顺达，力达刀尖，后手为勾。
（图4-43）

Key Points: The broadsword is thrusted from the waist, fast and powerful, with the force flowing and reaching the tip of the broadsword; the hand in the back is hooked. (Fig. 4-43)

图 4-43　弓步扎刀
Fig. 4-43 Broadsword Thrusting in a Bow Stance

练习刀术段前八级结束后行抱刀礼。

At the end of your practice, perform the broadsword-holding salute.

刀术段前九级　　Broadsword Play: Pre-Duan Level 9

刀术段前九级
Broadsword Play:
Pre-Duan Level 9

技术内容：刀法 + 步型 + 手型 + 腿法

（1）招数：11个动作。

（2）技法：10种（劈刀、扎刀、按刀、架刀、撩刀、缠头、藏刀、裹脑、截刀、带刀）。

（3）步型：7种（丁步、弓步、虚步、马步、仆步、歇步、后插步）。

（4）手型：1种（掌）。

（5）腿法：1种（箭踢）。

Technical Content: Broadsword Technique + Stance + Hand Form + Footwork

(1) Move: 11 moves.

(2) Technique: 10 techniques (broadsword chopping, thrusting, pressing, supporting, upper-cutting, coiling, concealing, wrapping, slashing, deflecting).

(3) Stance: 7 stances (T-Stance, bow stance, cat stance, horse stance, drop stance, resting stance, rear cross stance).

(4) Hand form: 1 hand form (palm).

(5) Footwork: 1 (arrow kicking).

练习刀术段前九级开始前行抱刀礼。

Before your practice, perform the broadsword-holding salute.

1. 预备势 Preparatory Posture

要点： 挺胸抬头，气息平稳，精神饱满，目视前方。（图4-44）

Key Points: Keep your chest up and breathe steadily; stay energetic and look straight ahead. (Fig. 4-44)

图 4-44　预备势
Fig. 4-44　Preparatory Posture

2. 丁步劈刀 Broadsword Chopping in a T-Stance

要点： 右下方劈刀，劈刀、手掌、丁步同时到位，力达刀刃。（图4-45）

Key Points: Chop from the lower right; the chopping, your palm, and the T-Stance are all in place simultaneously; the force reaches the blade. (Fig. 4-45)

图 4-45　丁步劈刀
Fig. 4-45　Broadsword Chopping in a T-Stance

3. 弓步扎刀　　　　　　　　Broadsword Thrusting in a Bow Stance

要点：扎刀迅速，劲力顺达，力达刀尖，弓步与扎刀动作一致。（图4-46）

Key Points: Perform the thrusting swiftly; keep the force flowing, with it reaching the tip of the blade; keep the bow stance consistent with the thrusting. (Fig. 4-46)

图 4-46　弓步扎刀
Fig. 4-46 Broadsword Thrusting in a Bow Stance

4. 虚步按刀　　　　　　　　Broadsword Pressing in a Cat Stance

要点：以腰带动，刀走立圆，小震脚呈虚步按刀，力达刀刃。（图4-47）

Key Points: Driven by your waist, the broadsword moves in a vertical circle; stamp your feet lightly and press the broadsword in a cat stance, with the force reaching the blade. (Fig. 4-47)

图 4-47　虚步按刀
Fig. 4-47 Broadsword Pressing in a Cat Stance

5. 提膝架刀　　　　　　　Broadsword Supporting with a Knee Up

要点：起身迅速，提膝平稳，刀架于头顶正上方，手腕用力。（图4-48）

Key Points: Get up quickly, raise your knee steadily, support the broadsword right above your head, and use your wrist to exert force. (Fig. 4-48)

图 4-48　提膝架刀
Fig. 4-48 Broadsword Supporting with a Knee Up

6. 上步前撩　　　　　　　Forward Upper-cutting in a Forward Stance

要点：手腕松活，以腰带臂，用力柔和，力达刀刃前部。（图4-49）

Key Points: Keep your wrist relaxed and flexible and use your waist to drive your arm; the force is gentle and reaches the front of the blade. (Fig. 4-49)

图 4-49　上步前撩
Fig. 4-49 Forward Upper-cutting in a Forward Stance

7. 后插步反撩　　　　　　　Reverse Upper-cutting in a Rear Cross Stance

要点：动作舒展，撩刀贴身，重心平稳，力达刀刃。（图4-50）

Key Points: Execute the movement with your body stretched, perform the upper-cutting with the broadsword close to the body, and keep the center of gravity stable, with the force reaching the blade. (Fig. 4-50)

图 4-50　后插步反撩
Fig. 4-50 Reverse Upper-cutting in a Rear Cross Stance

8. 马步平劈　　　　　　　Horizontal Chopping in a Horse Stance

要点：转身、马步、劈刀、摆头同时进行，挂刀贴身走立圆，劈刀力达刀刃。（图4-51）

Key Points: Turn around, stand in a horse stance, perform the chopping, and swing your head simultaneously; hang the broadsword and wield it in a vertical circle, and the force of chopping reaches the edge of the blade. (Fig. 4-51)

图 4-51　马步平劈
Fig. 4-51 Horizontal Chopping in a Horse Stance

9. 缠头箭踢藏刀　　　　Broadsword Coiling Followed by Arrow Kicking and Broadsword Concealing

要点： 箭踢须左脚蹬地、干净有力，重心保持稳定。（图4-52）

Key Points: The arrow kicking must be done with your right foot on the ground, and should be clean and powerful; keep your center of gravity stable. (Fig. 4-52)

图 4-52　缠头箭踢藏刀
Fig. 4-52　Broadsword Coiling Followed by Arrow Kicking and Broadsword Concealing

10. 裹脑歇步截刀　　　　Broadsword Wrapping Followed by Slashing in a Resting Stance

要点： 裹脑由缠头刀接歇步截刀，截刀力达刀刃，刀法与步法协调，歇步臀坐脚跟。（图4-53）

Key Points: The wrapping is followed by slashing in a resting stance, and the force reaches the edge of the blade; keep the broadsword movement and footwork coordinated; sit with hips on your heels when in a resting stance. (Fig. 4-53)

图 4-53　裹脑歇步截刀
Fig. 4-53　Broadsword Wrapping Followed by Slashing in a Resting Stance

11. 弓步平劈　　　　　　　Horizontal Broadsword Chopping in a Bow Stance

要点：刀走立圆，劈刀与弓步同时完成，眼随刀动，力达刀刃。（图4-54）

Key Points: The broadsword moves in a vertical circle; the chopping and bow stance are done simultaneously; your eyes move with the broadsword, and the force reaches the blade. (Fig. 4-54)

图 4-54　弓步平劈
Fig. 4-54 Horizontal Broadsword Chopping in a Bow Stance

12. 仆步带刀　　　　　　　Broadsword Deflecting in a Drop Stance

要点：以腰带臂，以肘带刀，动作敏捷，仆腿有力。（图4-55）

Key Points: Use your waist to drive your arms, and elbow to drive the broadsword; keep the movements swift; stretch your leg with force when in a drop stance. (Fig. 4-55)

图 4-55　仆步带刀
Fig. 4-55 Broadsword Deflecting in a Drop Stance

练习刀术段前九级结束后行抱刀礼。

At the end of your practice, perform the broadsword-holding salute.

刀术段位
考评技术内容
Duanwei Grading System for
Broadsword Play

一段刀术

一段刀术
Broadsword Play:
Grade 1

技术内容

（1）招数：15 式。

（2）段数：2 段。

（3）技法：14 种（扎刀、撩腕花、崩刀、点刀、挂刀、按刀、劈刀、架刀、撩刀、缠头刀、扫刀、裹脑刀、藏刀、抱刀）。

（4）步型：6 种（马步、弓步、歇步、后插步、虚步、丁步）。

（5）手型：1 种（掌）。

Technical Content

(1) Move: 15 moves.

(2) Section: 2 sections.

(3) Technique: 14 techniques (broadsword thrusting, spinning, upward poking, downward poking, hanging, pressing, chopping, supporting, upper-cutting, coiling, sweeping, wrapping, concealing, holding).

(4) Stance: 6 stances (horse stance, bow stance, resting stance, rear cross stance, cat stance, T-Stance).

(5) Hand form: 1 hand form (palm).

动作名称

1. 起势（并步举抱刀）
2. 弓步扎刀
3. 撩腕花丁步崩刀
4. 弓步点刀
5. 提膝挂刀
6. 右转身挂刀
7. 歇步按刀
8. 马步劈刀
9. 提膝架刀
10. 上步撩刀
11. 后插步反撩
12. 转身缠头刀
13. 歇步扫刀
14. 裹脑虚步藏刀
15. 收势（并步抱刀）

Names of the Moves

1. Starting Position (Broadsword Holding and Supporting with Feet Together)
2. Broadsword Thrusting in a Bow Stance
3. Broadsword Spinning Followed by Upward Poking in a T-Stance
4. Broadsword Downward Poking in a Bow Stance
5. Broadsword Hanging with a Knee Up
6. Broadsword Hanging After Turning Right
7. Broadsword Pressing in a Resting Stance
8. Broadsword Chopping in a Horse Stance
9. Broadsword Supporting with a Knee Up
10. Stepping Forward for Broadsword Upper-cutting
11. Reverse Upper-cutting in a Rear Cross Stance
12. Turning Around for Broadsword Coiling
13. Broadsword Sweeping in a Resting Stance
14. Broadsword Wrapping Followed by Concealing in a Cat Stance
15. Closing Posture (Broadsword Holding with Feet Together)

练习一段刀术开始前行抱刀礼。

Before your practice, perform the broadsword-holding salute.

1. 起势（并步举抱刀） Starting Position (Broadsword Holding and Supporting with Feet Together)

要点： 上步、并步迅速，双手上举，交合于头顶正上方。（图5-1）

Key Points: Step forward and keep your feet together quickly; raise your hands and let them meet above your head. (Fig. 5-1)

图 5-1　起势（并步举抱刀）
Fig. 5-1 Starting Position(Broadsword Holding and Supporting with Feet Together)

2. 弓步扎刀 Broadsword Thrusting in a Bow Stance

要点： 扎刀迅速，劲力顺达，力达刀尖。（图5-2）

Key Points: Perform the thrusting swiftly; keep the force flowing, with the force reaching the tip of the blade. (Fig. 5-2)

图 5-2　弓步扎刀
Fig. 5-2 Broadsword Thrusting in a Bow Stance

3. 撩腕花丁步崩刀

Broadsword Spinning Followed by Upward Poking in a T-Stance

要点：撤步迅速，撩腕花立圆贴身，崩刀力达刀尖。（图5-3）

Key Points: Withdraw your feet quickly; perform the spinning and then keep the broadsword close to your body and move it in a vertical circle; the force of upward poking reaches the tip of the blade. (Fig. 5-3)

图 5-3　撩腕花丁步崩刀
Fig. 5-3 Broadsword Spinning Followed by Upward Poking in a T-Stance

4. 弓步点刀

Broadsword Downward Poking in a Bow Stance

要点：跨步稳健，提腕快速，力达刀尖。（图5-4）

Key Points: Step forward steadily; lift your wrist up swiftly, with the force reaching the tip of the blade. (Fig. 5-4)

图 5-4　弓步点刀
Fig. 5-4 Broadsword Downward Poking in a Bow Stance

5. 提膝挂刀　　　　　　　　　　　Broadsword Hanging with a Knee Up

要点：挂刀贴身，腕部扣紧，刀尖先行，力达刀背。（图5-5）

Key Points: Hang the broadsword close to the body, and keep your wrist tight; the tip of the blade moves first, and the force reaches the spine of the blade. (Fig. 5-5)

图 5-5　提膝挂刀
Fig. 5-5 Broadsword Hanging with a Knee Up

6. 右转身挂刀　　　　　　　　Broadsword Hanging After Turning Right

要点：转身稳健，挂刀贴身，身械协调，力达刀背。（图5-6）

Key Points: Turn around steadily and hang the broadsword close to the body; coordinate your body and the broadsword, and the force reaches the spine of the blade. (Fig. 5-6)

图 5-6　右转身挂刀
Fig. 5-6 Broadsword Hanging After Turning Right

7. 歇步按刀   Broadsword Pressing in a Resting Stance

要点：步法轻快，落地稳定，按刀接近地面，力达刀刃。（图5-7）

Key Points: Keep your footwork brisk before a stable landing; keep the broadsword close to the ground, with the force reaching the blade. (Fig. 5-7)

图 5-7　歇步按刀

Fig. 5-7 Broadsword Pressing in a Resting Stance

8. 马步劈刀   Broadsword Chopping in a Horse Stance

要点：以腰为轴，转身后自上而下劈刀，力达刀刃。（图5-8）

Key Points: With your waist as the axis, turn around and perform the chopping from top to bottom, with the force reaching the blade. (Fig. 5-8)

图 5-8　马步劈刀

Fig. 5-8 Broadsword Chopping in a Horse Stance

9. 提膝架刀   Broadsword Supporting with a Knee Up

要点：刀刃向上，右腿蹬地，左腿提膝同时架刀，力达刀刃。（图5-9）

Key Points: The blade faces upward, and your right leg stays on the ground; raise your left knee while performing the broadsword supporting, with the force reaching the blade. (Fig. 5-9)

图 5-9　提膝架刀
Fig. 5-9 Broadsword Supporting with a Knee Up

10. 上步撩刀   Stepping Forward for Broadsword Upper-cutting

要点：手腕松活，以腰带臂，用力柔和，力达刀刃前部。（图5-10）

Key Points: Relax your wrist and use your waist to drive your arm; exert force gently, and the force reaches the front of the blade. (Fig. 5-10)

图 5-10　上步撩刀

Fig. 5-10　Stepping Forward for Broadsword Upper-cutting

11. 后插步反撩　　　　　　　　Reverse Upper-cutting in a Rear Cross Stance

要点：动作舒展，撩刀贴身，重心平稳，力达刀刃。（图5—11）

Key Points: Execute the movement with your body stretched, perform the upper-cutting with the broadsword close to the body, and keep the center of gravity stable, with the force reaching the blade. (Fig. 5-11)

图 5-11　后插步反撩

Fig. 5-11　Reverse Upper-cutting in a Rear Cross Stance

12. 转身缠头刀   Turning Around for Broadsword Coiling

要点：重心稳定，缠头时刀背紧贴身体，环绕时不得触碰头部，动作干净利落。（图5-12）

Key Points: Keep your center of gravity stable; when performing the coiling, the spine of the blade stays close to your body, but should not touch your head; keep the movement coherent and neat. (Fig. 5-12)

图 5-12　转身缠头刀
Fig. 5-12 Turning Around for Broadsword Coiling

13. 歇步扫刀   Broadsword Sweeping in a Resting Stance

要点：顺身体旋转之势，扫刀动作一气呵成，刀身要平，与膝同高。
（图5-13）

Key Points: As you turn your body, perform the sweeping without interruption, with the blade staying flat at the knee level. (Fig. 5-13)

图 5-13　歇步扫刀
Fig. 5-13 Broadsword Sweeping in a Resting Stance

14. 裹脑虚步藏刀　　　　Broadsword Wrapping Followed by Concealing in a Cat Stance

要点： 裹脑时刀背紧贴身体，虚步藏刀和推掌同时完成，力达刀身。（图5-14）

Key Points: When performing the wrapping, the spine of the broadsword stays close to your body; perform the concealing and push your palm at the same time, with the force reaching the blade. (Fig. 5-14)

图 5-14　裹脑虚步藏刀
Fig. 5-14 Broadsword Wrapping Followed by Concealing in a Cat Stance

15. 收势（并步抱刀） Closing Posture (Broadsword Holding with Feet Together)

要点：后退两步并一步，接刀左右协调配合，甩头精神饱满。（图5-15）

Key Points: Take two steps back and keep your feet together; take the broadsword in coordination with the left and right, and swing your head energetically. (Fig. 5-15)

图 5-15　收势（并步抱刀）
Fig. 5-15 Closing Posture (Broadsword Holding with Feet Together)

练习一段刀术结束后行抱刀礼。

At the end of your practice, perform the broadsword-holding salute.

二段刀术　　　　　Broadsword Play: Grade 2

二段刀术
Broadsword Play:
Grade 2

技术内容

（1）招数：18 式。

（2）段数：2 段。

（3）技法：13 种（缠头、裹脑、藏刀、扎刀、按刀、斩刀、劈刀、格刀、撩刀、带刀、推刀、砍刀、抱刀）。

（4）步型：6 种（马步、弓步、歇步、仆步、虚步、后插步）。

（5）手型：2 种（掌、勾）。

（6）腿法：1 种（蹬腿）。

Technical Content

(1) Move: 18 moves.

(2) Section: 2 sections.

(3) Technique: 13 techniques (broadsword coiling, wrapping, concealing, thrusting, pressing, hacking, chopping, blocking, upper-cutting, deflecting, pushing, cutting, holding).

(4) Stance: 6 stances (horse stance, bow stance, resting stance, drop stance, cat stance, rear cross stance).

(5) Hand form: 2 hand forms (palm, hook).

(6) Footwork: 1 (kicking).

动作名称

1. 起势（并步举抱刀）
2. 弓步藏刀
3. 虚步藏刀
4. 弓步扎刀
5. 弓步抢劈
6. 提膝格刀
7. 弓步推刀
8. 马步劈刀
9. 仆步按刀
10. 蹬腿藏刀
11. 弓步平斩
12. 弓步带刀
13. 歇步下砍
14. 弓步扎刀
15. 后插步反撩
16. 弓步藏刀
17. 虚步抱刀
18. 收势

Names of the Moves

1. Starting Position (Broadsword Holding and Supporting with Feet Together)
2. Broadsword Concealing in a Bow Stance
3. Broadsword Concealing in a Cat Stance
4. Broadsword Thrusting in a Bow Stance
5. Broadsword Swinging and Chopping in a Bow Stance
6. Broadsword Blocking with a Knee Up
7. Broadsword Pushing in a Bow Stance
8. Broadsword Chopping in a Horse Stance
9. Broadsword Pressing in a Drop Stance
10. Broadsword Concealing While Kicking a Leg
11. Horizontal Hacking in a Bow Stance
12. Broadsword Deflecting in a Bow Stance
13. Broadsword Downward Cutting in a Resting Stance
14. Broadsword Thrusting in a Bow Stance
15. Reverse Upper-cutting in a Rear Cross Stance
16. Broadsword Concealing in a Bow Stance
17. Broadsword Holding in a Cat Stance
18. Closing Posture

练习二段刀术开始前行抱刀礼。

Before your practice, perform the broadsword-holding salute.

1. 起势（并步举抱刀） Starting Position (Broadsword Holding and Supporting with Feet Together)

要点：并步，双手上举，交合于头顶正上方。（图5-16）

Key Points: Step forward and keep your feet together quickly; raise your hands and let them meet above your head. (Fig. 5-16)

图 5-16　起势（并步举抱刀）
Fig. 5-16 Starting Position (Broadsword Holding and Supporting with Feet Together)

2. 弓步藏刀 Broadsword Concealing in a Bow Stance

要点：刀背贴脊背绕行，快速成弓步，腋下藏刀，力达刀身。（图 5-17）

Key Points: The broadsword goes around with its blade spine close to your back; get into a bow stance swiftly and conceal the broadsword under the armpit, with the force reaching the blade. (Fig. 5-17)

刀术
Broadsword

图 5-17　弓步藏刀
Fig. 5-17 Broadsword Concealing in a Bow Stance

3. 虚步藏刀　　　　　　　　　　Broadsword Concealing in a Cat Stance

要点：先裹脑后藏刀，刀背与身体紧贴环绕，虚步成型，动作流畅。（图5-18）

Key Points: Perform the wrapping before concealing the broadsword; the blade spine stays close to the body; the movements are done in a cat stance, and should be coherent. (Fig. 5-18)

图 5-18　虚步藏刀
Fig. 5-18 Broadsword Concealing in a Cat Stance

4. 弓步扎刀　　　　　　　　　　Broadsword Thrusting in a Bow Stance

要点：左勾手，右扎刀；以腰部力量带动手臂持刀直刺，力达刀尖。（图5-19）

Key Points: Your left hand is hooked, and perform the thrusting with your right hand. Use the strength of your waist to drive your arm to hold the broadsword and perform the thrusting, with the force reaching the tip of the blade. (Fig. 5-19)

图 5-19　弓步扎刀
Fig. 5-19 Broadsword Thrusting in a Bow Stance

5. 弓步抡劈　　　　　　　Broadsword Swinging and Chopping in a Bow Stance

要点：上臂带动前臂下劈，动作连贯，步法配合，力达刀刃。（图 5-20）

Key Points: Swing your upper arm to drive the forearm from top to bottom; keep the movements coherent and coordinate your footwork; the force reaches the blade. (Fig. 5-20)

图 5-20　弓步抡劈
Fig. 5-20 Broadsword Swinging and Chopping in a Bow Stance

6. 提膝格刀   Broadsword Blocking with a Knee Up

要点：收刀，回头迅猛，眼到手到，提膝与格刀同步完成。（图5-21）

Key Points: Withdraw the broadsword and turn your head back quickly; eyes follow your hand; raise your knee and perform the blocking simultaneously. (Fig. 5-21)

图 5-21 　提膝格刀
Fig. 5-21 Broadsword Blocking with a Knee Up

7. 弓步推刀   Broadsword Pushing in a Bow Stance

要点：顺势迅速上步，身体前倾，双臂同时向前发力将刀推出，力达刀刃。（图5-22）

Key Points: Step forward quickly, lean forward, and push the broadsword forward with both arms exerting force, which reaches the edge of the blade. (Fig. 5-22)

图 5-22 　弓步推刀
Fig. 5-22 Broadsword Pushing in a Bow Stance

8. 马步劈刀　　　　　　　　　　Broadsword Chopping in a Horse Stance

要点：腰部带动手臂下劈，刀必须举过头顶，干脆迅猛，力达刀身。
（图5-23）

Key Points: Use your waist to drive your arm to chop downward; the broadsword must be raised above your head; the movement should be neat and forceful, with the force reaching the blade. (Fig. 5-23)

图 5-23　马步劈刀
Fig. 5-23　Broadsword Chopping in a Horse Stance

9. 仆步按刀　　　　　　　　　　Broadsword Pressing in a Drop Stance

要点：右脚后撤同时撩腕花，呈仆步按刀，刀刃向下，目视刀尖方向。（图5-24）

Key Points: Step back with your right foot while performing the spinning; press the broadsword in a drop stance, with the blade facing downward, and eyes on where the tip of the blade is pointing. (Fig. 5-24)

图 5-24　仆步按刀
Fig. 5-24　Broadsword Pressing in a Drop Stance

10. 蹬腿藏刀   Broadsword Concealing While Kicking a Leg

要点：缠头时刀背紧贴身体，藏于肋下，同时提膝蹬腿，一气呵成，力达脚跟。（图5-25）

Key Points: When performing the coiling, keep the spine of the blade close to the body; conceal the broadsword below the ribs, and raise your knee to kick your leg in one go, with the force reaching the heel. (Fig. 5-25)

图 5-25　蹬腿藏刀
Fig. 5-25 Broadsword Concealing While Kicking a Leg

11. 弓步平斩   Horizontal Hacking in a Bow Stance

要点：转身缠头动作须协调一致，以腰为轴，带动四肢，平斩力达刀刃。（图5-26）

Key Points: The movements of turning around and broadsword coiling must be coordinated; use your waist as the axis to drive the limbs, with the force of horizontal hacking reaching the blade. (Fig. 5-26)

图 5-26　弓步平斩
Fig. 5-26 Horizontal Hacking in a Bow Stance

12. 弓步带刀　　　　　　　　Broadsword Deflecting in a Bow Stance

要点： 弓步变换灵活，后带动作连贯，目视右侧。（图5-27）

Key Points: Change your bow stance flexibly, keep the subsequent movements coherent, and look to the right side. (Fig. 5-27)

图 5-27　弓步带刀
Fig. 5-27 Broadsword Deflecting in a Bow Stance

13. 歇步下砍　　　　　　Broadsword Downward Cutting in a Resting Stance

要点： 臀部坐在左小腿，身体略微前倾，目视刀身；下砍时，力达刀身后段。（图5-28）

Key Points: Sit on your left calf, leaning forward slightly and looking at the blade; when cutting downward, the force reaches the lower part of the blade. (Fig. 5-28)

图 5-28　歇步下砍
Fig. 5-28 Broadsword Downward Cutting in a Resting Stance

14. 弓步扎刀   Broadsword Thrusting in a Bow Stance

要点：身体左转，腰部带动，弓步与扎刀同时完成，扎刀迅猛，力达刀尖。（图5-29）

Key Points: Turn your body to the left; driven by your waist, get into a bow stance and perform the thrusting simultaneously; the movement should be swift and powerful, and the force reaches the tip of the blade. (Fig. 5-29)

图 5-29 弓步扎刀
Fig. 5-29 Broadsword Thrusting in a Bow Stance

15. 后插步反撩   Reverse Upper-cutting in a Rear Cross Stance

要点：上步撩刀接后插步反撩，身体前倾，撩刀贴身走立圆，力达刀刃。（图5-30）

Key Points: Step forward, and then get into a rear cross stance to perform the reverse upper-cutting; lean forward, and the broadsword goes in a vertical circle, with the force reaching the edge of the blade. (Fig. 5-30)

图 5-30 后插步反撩
Fig. 5-30 Reverse Upper-cutting in a Rear Cross Stance

16. 弓步藏刀   Broadsword Concealing in a Bow Stance

要点：缠头刀背须贴脊背绕行，弓步和藏刀同时完成，藏刀力达刀身。（图5–31）

Key Points: When performing the coiling, the spine of the blade must stay close to your back; get into a bow stance and perform the concealing simultaneously, with the force reaching the blade. (Fig. 5-31)

图 5–31　弓步藏刀
Fig. 5-31　Broadsword Concealing in a Bow Stance

17. 虚步抱刀   Broadsword Holding in a Cat Stance

要点：持刀顺势臂外旋做裹脑动作，接刀时左右手相互配合，摆头与抖腕同步。（图5–32）

Key Points: Hold the broadsword and perform the wrapping; when receiving the broadsword, your left and right hands coordinate with each other; swing your head and wrist simultaneously. (Fig. 5-32)

图 5–32　虚步抱刀
Fig. 5-32　Broadsword Holding in a Cat Stance

18. 收势 Closing Posture

要点： 并步还原，抱刀立正，精神饱满。（图5-33）

Key Points: Stand with feet together, hold the broadsword and stand at attention spirited. (Fig. 5-33)

图 5-33　收势
Fig. 5-33　Closing Posture

练习二段刀术结束后行抱刀礼。

At the end of your practice, perform the broadsword-holding salute.

三段刀术（初级刀术） Broadsword Play: Grade 3 (Primary Broadsword Play)

三段刀术
Broadsword Play:
Grade 3

技术内容

（1）招数：34式。

（2）段数：4段。

（3）技法：14种（缠头、裹脑、扎刀、挑刀、劈刀、撩刀、斩刀、带刀、砍刀、按刀、藏刀、撩刀、扫刀、抱刀）。

（4）步型：6种（马步、弓步、歇步、仆步、虚步、后插步）。

（5）手型：2种（掌、勾）。

（6）腿法：2个（蹬腿、箭踢）。

（7）跳跃：1个。

Technical Content

(1) Move: 34 moves.

(2) Section: 4 sections.

(3) Technique: 14 techniques (broadsword coiling, wrapping, thrusting, upward slitting, chopping, upper-cutting, hacking, deflecting, cutting, pressing, concealing, upper-cutting, sweeping, holding).

(4) Stance: 6 stances (horse stance, bow stance, resting stance, drop stance, cat stance, rear cross stance).

(5) Hand form: 2 hand forms (palm, hook).

(6) Footwork: 2 (kicking, arrow kicking).

(7) Jump: 1 jump.

动作名称

1. 起势
2. 弓步缠头
3. 虚步藏刀
4. 弓步扎刀
5. 并步上挑
6. 左抡劈
7. 右抡劈
8. 弓步撩刀
9. 弓步藏刀
10. 提膝缠头
11. 弓步平斩
12. 仆步带刀
13. 歇步下砍
14. 左劈刀
15. 右劈刀
16. 歇步按刀
17. 马步劈刀
18. 弓步撩刀
19. 插步反撩
20. 转身挂劈
21. 仆步下砍
22. 架刀前刺
23. 左斜劈
24. 右斜劈

25. 虚步藏刀
26. 旋转扫刀
27. 翻身劈刀
28. 缠头箭踢
29. 仆步按刀
30. 缠头蹬腿
31. 虚步藏刀
32. 弓步缠头
33. 并步抱刀
34. 收势（并步抱刀）

Names of the Moves

1. Starting Position

2. Broadsword Coiling in a Bow Stance

3. Broadsword Concealing in a Cat Stance

4. Broadsword Thrusting in a Bow Stance

5. Upward Slitting with Feet Together

6. Left Swinging and Chopping

7. Right Swinging and Chopping

8. Broadsword Upper-cutting in a Bow Stance

9. Broadsword Concealing in a Bow Stance

10. Broadsword Coiling with a Knee Up

11. Horizontal Hacking in a Bow Stance

12. Broadsword Deflecting in a Drop Stance

13. Broadsword Downward Cutting in a Resting Stance

14. Left Chopping

15. Right Chopping

16. Broadsword Pressing in a Resting Stance

17. Broadsword Chopping in a Horse Stance

18. Broadsword Upper-cutting in a Bow Stance

19. Reverse Upper-cutting in a Rear Cross Stance

20. Turning Around for Broadsword Hanging and Chopping

21. Broadsword Downward Cutting in a Drop Stance

22. Broadsword Supporting and Thrusting Forward

23. Slanted Chopping to the Left

24. Slanted Chopping to the Right

25. Broadsword Concealing in a Cat Stance

26. Rotating for Broadsword Sweeping

27. Turning over for Broadsword Chopping

28. Broadsword Coiling Followed by Arrow Kicking

29. Broadsword Pressing in a Drop Stance

30. Broadsword Coiling and Kicking

31. Broadsword Concealing in a Cat Stance

32. Broadsword Coiling in a Bow Stance

33. Broadsword Holding with Feet Together

34. Closing Posture (Broadsword Holding with Feet Together)

练习三段刀术开始前行抱刀礼。

Before your practice, perform the broadsword-holding salute.

要点：虚步抱刀，挺胸、塌腰，并步抱刀上半步、进一步和并步动作连贯。（图5–34）

Key Points: Hold the broadsword in a cat stance, with your chest up and waist inward; support and hold the broadsword with feet together, and then step half a step forward, step further, and stand with feet together; keep these movements coherent. (Fig. 5-34)

图 5–34 　起势
Fig. 5-34 Starting Position

要点：缠头刀背须贴脊背绕行，左手配合，刀背贴左肋，刀尖向后。（图5–35）

Key Points: When performing the coiling, keep the blade spine close to your back; your left hand should be well coordinated, and the blade spine should be attached to your left rib, with the tip of the blade facing backward. (Fig. 5-35)

图 5-35　弓步缠头

Fig. 5-35 Broadsword Coiling in a Bow Stance

3. 虚步藏刀　　　　　　　　　　　Broadsword Concealing in a Cat Stance

要点： 裹脑时，刀背与身体背部紧贴环绕，动作流畅，藏刀手腕用刀。（图5-36）

Key Points: When performing the wrapping, keep the blade spine close to your back, and keep the movements flowing; when concealing the broadsword, use your wrist to exert force. (Fig. 5-36)

图 5-36　虚步藏刀

Fig. 5-36 Broadsword Concealing in a Cat Stance

4. 弓步扎刀   Broadsword Thrusting in a Bow Stance

要点： 上步，以腰带动弓步扎刀，左勾右扎，力达刀尖。（图5-37）

Key Points: Step forward, use your waist to drive the thrusting in a bow stance; your left hand is hooked and perform the thrusting with your right hand, with the force reaching the tip of the blade. (Fig. 5-37)

图 5-37　弓步扎刀
Fig. 5-37 Broadsword Thrusting in a Bow Stance

5. 并步上挑   Upward Slitting with Feet Together

要点： 后退、并步、上挑，收腹挺胸，手腕上抖发力，刀尖向下。（图5-38）

Key Points: Step back and perform the upward slitting with feet together, with your abdomen in and chest up; sway your wrist upward to exert force, and the tip of the blade points downward. (Fig. 5-38)

图 5-38　并步上挑
Fig. 5-38 Upward Slitting with Feet Together

6. 左抡劈 Left Swinging and Chopping

要点： 刀举过头顶自上向下劈，动作连贯、有力，与步法配合一致。
（图5-39）

Key Points: Raise the broadsword above your head and chop from top to bottom; keep the movements coherent, powerful, and coordinated with your footwork. (Fig. 5-39)

图 5-39　左抡劈
Fig. 5-39 Left Swinging and Chopping

7. 右抡劈 Right Swinging and Chopping

要点： 右手持刀经过头顶向前劈，力达刀身，步法与刀法协调一致。
（图5-40）

Key Points: Use your right hand to hold the broadsword above your head and chop forward, with the force reaching the blade; coordinate the movements with footwork. (Fig. 5-40)

图 5-40　右抡劈
Fig. 5-40 Right Swinging and Chopping

8. 弓步撩刀 Broadsword Upper-cutting in a Bow Stance

要点：撩刀以腰为轴，带动四肢，上下肢协调配合，刀尖斜向下。（图5-41）

Key Points: When performing the upper-cutting, use your waist as the axis to drive the limbs; coordinate your upper and lower limbs, and the tip of the blade is tilted downward. (Fig. 5-41)

图 5-41　弓步撩刀
Fig. 5-41 Broadsword Upper-cutting in a Bow Stance

9. 弓步藏刀 Broadsword Concealing in a Bow Stance

要点：裹脑紧贴背部环绕，转身协调，刀身贴近右腿，刀尖藏于膝旁。（图5-42）

Key Points: Perform the wrapping with the broadsword close to your back, and turn around to coordinate the movements; when concealing the broadsword, keep the blade of the broadsword close to the right leg, and the tip of the blade is concealed by the knee. (Fig. 5-42)

图 5-42　弓步藏刀
Fig. 5-42 Broadsword Concealing in a Bow Stance

10. 提膝缠头　　　　　　　　　Broadsword Coiling with a Knee Up

要点：缠头时刀背与身体紧贴环绕，提膝与缠头动作同步完成，支撑腿五趾抓地。（图5-43）

Key Points: When performing the coiling, keep the blade spine close to your body; raise your knee and perform the coiling simultaneously, and the toes of the supporting leg stay firm to the ground. (Fig. 5-43)

图 5-43　提膝缠头
Fig. 5-43 Broadsword Coiling with a Knee Up

11. 弓步平斩　　　　　　　　Horizontal Hacking in a Bow Stance

要点：以腰为核心，带动腿部和手臂发力，平斩力达刀刃。（图5-44）

Key Points: Your waist works as the core and drives your legs and arms to exert force, which reaches the blade. (Fig. 5-44)

图 5-44　弓步平斩
Fig. 5-44 Horizontal Hacking in a Bow Stance

12. 仆步带刀　　　　　　　　　　Broadsword Deflecting in a Drop Stance

要点：步型变换要灵活，带刀动作要连贯，下肢稳定。（图5-45）

Key Points: Change your footwork and stance flexibly; keep the movements of broadsword deflecting coherent, and your lower limbs stable. (Fig. 5-45)

图 5-45　仆步带刀
Fig. 5-45　Broadsword Deflecting in a Drop Stance

13. 歇步下砍　　　　　　Broadsword Downward Cutting in a Resting Stance

要点：移动重心，同时做裹脑动作，随即歇步下砍，力达刀身后段。
（图5-46）

Key Points: Move the center of gravity and perform the wrapping simultaneously; then get into a resting stance and chop down, with the force reaching the lower part of the blade. (Fig. 5-46)

图 5-46　歇步下砍
Fig. 5-46　Broadsword Downward Cutting in a Resting Stance

14. 左劈刀 Left Chopping

要点：腰部拧转带动腿部旋转，顺旋转惯性向左下劈刀，力达刀刃。（图5-47）

Key Points: Turn your waist to drive the legs to rotate, and as your legs rotate, chop down to the left, with the force reaching the blade. (Fig. 5-47)

图 5-47　左劈刀
Fig. 5-47　Left Chopping

15. 右劈刀 Right Chopping

要点：与左劈刀相同，向右下劈刀，力达刀刃。（图5-48）

Key Points: This move is similar to left chopping. The difference is that you chop down to the right, with the force reaching the blade. (Fig. 5-48)

图 5-48　右劈刀
Fig. 5-48　Right Chopping

16. 歇步按刀   Broadsword Pressing in a Resting Stance

要点：保持重心稳定，插步、歇步、绕刀、按刀快速连贯，力达刀刃。（图5-49）

Key Points: Keep your center of gravity balanced; the movements of getting into a cross stance and resting stance, broadsword spinning and pressing should be quick and coherent, and the force reaches the blade. (Fig. 5-49)

图 5-49 歇步按刀
Fig. 5-49 Broadsword Pressing in a Resting Stance

17. 马步劈刀   Broadsword Chopping in a Horse Stance

要点：转身以腰为轴，劈刀自上而下，迅猛用力，力达刀身。（图5-50）

Key Points: Turn around and use the waist as the axis; perform the chopping from top to bottom, and the force reaches the blade. (Fig. 5-50)

图 5-50 马步劈刀
Fig. 5-50 Broadsword Chopping in a Horse Stance

18. 弓步撩刀   Broadsword Upper-cutting in a Bow Stance

要点：撩刀要贴身，刀刃斜向上，刀尖斜向下，力达刀刃前部。（图 5-51）

Key Points: When performing the upper-cutting, keep the broadsword close to the body, with the blade tilted upward, the tip of the blade tilted downward, and the force reaching the front of the blade. (Fig. 5-51)

图 5-51 弓步撩刀
Fig. 5-51 Broadsword Upper-cutting in a Bow Stance

19. 插步反撩   Reverse Upper-cutting in a Rear Cross Stance

要点：撩刀贴身，路线走立圆，幅度大，动作连贯，力达刀刃，眼随刀动。（图5-52）

Key Points: When performing the upper-cutting, keep the broadsword close to the body and move it in a vertical circle with a large range of movements, which should be coherent; the force reaches the blade, and your eyes move with the broadsword. (Fig. 5-52)

图 5-52 插步反撩
Fig. 5-52 Reverse Upper-cutting in a Rear Cross Stance

20. 转身挂劈　　　Turning Around for Broadsword Hanging and Chopping

要点： 挂刀时屈腕、贴身，挂劈要连贯，劈刀力达刀刃。（图5-53）

Key Points: When hanging the broadsword, bend your wrist and keep the broadsword close to the body; keep the hanging and chopping coherent, and the force of chopping should reach the blade. (Fig. 5-53)

图 5-53　转身挂劈

Fig. 5-53 Turning Around for Broadsword Hanging and Chopping

21. 仆步下砍　　　Broadsword Downward Cutting in a Drop Stance

要点： 砍刀时顺裹脑之势发力，力达刀刃，与仆步同时完成。（图5-54）

Key Points: When performing the chopping, follow the wrapping to exert force, and the force reaches the blade. Complete the chopping and get into a drop stance simultaneously. (Fig. 5-54)

图 5-54 仆步下砍
Fig. 5-54 Broadsword Downward Cutting in a Drop Stance

22. 架刀前刺   Broadsword Supporting and Thrusting Forward

要点：以脚掌为轴蹍地，架刀提膝迅速连贯；刺刀劲力充足，力达刀尖。（图5-55）

Key Points: With the sole of the foot as the axis, gently rub your foot against the ground; perform the broadsword supporting and raise your knee quickly and coherently; the force of the thrusting should suffice to reach the tip of the blade. (Fig. 5-55)

图 5-55 架刀前刺
Fig. 5-55 Broadsword Supporting and Thrusting Forward

23. 左斜劈 {#23}   Slanted Chopping to the Left

要点：顺缠头之势向左下斜劈，力达刀刃前部，斜劈快速有力。（图5-56）

Key Points: Follow the movement of wrapping to chop down to the left, with the force reaching the front of the blade; this movement should be swift and powerful. (Fig. 5-56)

图 5-56　左斜劈
Fig. 5-56 Slanted Chopping to the Left

24. 右斜劈 {#24}   Slanted Chopping to the Right

要点：以腰为轴转身斜劈，劈刀同时提右膝，力达刀刃。（图5-57）

Key Points: Use your waist as the axis, turn around and chop diagonally, raising your right knee at the same time; the force reaches the blade. (Fig. 5-57)

图 5-57　右斜劈
Fig. 5-57 Slanted Chopping to the Right

25. 虚步藏刀　　　　　　　　Broadsword Concealing in a Cat Stance

要点：由裹脑衔接，刀背贴靠脊背绕行，藏刀扣腕，步型与动作同步完成。（图5-58）

Key Points: This move follows the wrapping, with the blade spine staying close to your back and going in circles. Conceal the broadsword and keep your wrist tight; get into a cat stance and finish the move simultaneously. (Fig. 5-58)

图 5-58　虚步藏刀
Fig. 5-58 Broadsword Concealing in a Cat Stance

26. 旋转扫刀　　　　　　　　Rotating for Broadsword Sweeping

要点：由缠头衔接，刀背须贴身，借旋转之势，动作一气呵成，刀身要平。（图5-59）

Key Points: This move follows the coiling. Keep the blade spine close to your body. With the rotation, complete the movements in one go, and keep the blade in a flat position. (Fig. 5-59)

图 5-59　旋转扫刀
Fig. 5-59 Rotating for Broadsword Sweeping

27. 翻身劈刀   *Turning over for Broadsword Chopping*

要点：翻身跃步，抡劈立圆，身体随刀法上举和下劈运动，协调一致，劈刀力达刀刃。（图5-60）

Key Points: Turn over and jump, perform the swinging and chopping, with the broadsword going in a circle, and your body moves up and down with the broadsword; keep the movements in harmony, and the force of chopping reaches the blade. (Fig. 5-60)

图 5-60　翻身劈刀
Fig. 5-60 Turning over for Broadsword Chopping

28. 缠头箭踢   Broadsword Coiling Followed by Arrow Kicking

要点：缠头和箭踢先后协调进行，缠头快速，箭踢有力，膝关节伸直。（图5-61）

Key Points: The coiling and arrow kicking are done successively with coordination. Keep the coiling fast, and the arrow kicking powerful; keep the knee straight. (Fig. 5-61)

图 5-61　缠头箭踢
Fig. 5-61 Broadsword Coiling Followed by Arrow Kicking

29. 仆步按刀   Broadsword Pressing in a Drop Stance

要点：裹脑动作在空中完成，仆步按刀双手用力，力达刀刃。（图 5-62）

Key Points: Complete the wrapping in the air; when pressing the broadsword in a drop stance, exert force with both hands, and the force reaches the blade. (Fig. 5-62)

图 5-62　仆步按刀
Fig. 5-62　Broadsword Pressing in a Drop Stance

30. 缠头蹬腿   Broadsword Coiling and Kicking

要点：由提膝、左弓步过渡到缠头蹬腿，动作要连贯，蹬腿力达脚跟。（图5-63）

Key Points: The move transitions from raising your knee and a left bow stance to broadsword coiling and kicking a leg. Keep the movements coherent, and the kicking force should reach the heel. (Fig. 5-63)

图 5-63　缠头蹬腿
Fig. 5-63　Broadsword Coiling and Kicking

31. 虚步藏刀   Broadsword Concealing in a Cat Stance

要点：转身动作轻快敏捷，与裹脑绕背协调一致，以腰为轴，动作蓄发有力。（图5-64）

Key Points: Turn around briskly, and keep the movement in harmony with broadsword wrapping. With the waist as the axis, the movements should be forceful. (Fig. 5-64)

图 5-64　虚步藏刀
Fig. 5-64 Broadsword Concealing in a Cat Stance

32. 弓步缠头   Broadsword Coiling in a Bow Stance

要点：缠头刀背贴背脊绕行，上下肢协调一致，快速有力，力达刀身。（图5-65）

Key Points: When performing the coiling, keep the blade spine close to your back, and cocrdinate your upper and lower limbs. Keep the movements swift and powerful, and the force reaches the blade. (Fig. 5-65)

图 5-65　弓步缠头
Fig. 5-65 Broadsword Coiling in a Bow Stance

33. 并步抱刀　　　　　　　　　　　Broadsword Holding with Feet Together

要点：接刀时左右手配合，并步与接刀动作协调一致，挺胸收腹。
（图5–66）

Key Points: When taking the broadsword, your left hand works with the right one; standing with feet together should be coordinated with the broadsword-taking, with your chest up and abdomen in. (Fig. 5-66)

图 5–66　并步抱刀
Fig. 5-66 Broadsword Holding with Feet Together

34. 收势（并步抱刀）　　　Closing Posture (Broadsword Holding with Feet Together)

要点：后退与绕掌配合协调，眼随手动，摆头按掌迅速，双目有神。
（图5–67）

Key Points: Stepping backward and swinging palms are coordinated; eyes move with your hands; swing your head and press your palm swiftly, and your eyes should look bright and piercing. (Fig. 5-67)

图 5-67　收势（并步抱刀）
Fig. 5-67 Closing Posture (Broadsword Holding with Feet Together)

练习三段刀术结束后行抱刀礼。

At the end of your practice, perform the broadsword-holding salute.